D1166613

"With stinging humor, penetrating insight, and her trademark directness, Shulman has crafted a narrative that rings with truth on every page of this gorgeous book."   —Dani Shapiro, author of *Slow Motion*

"Fascinating. . . . Shulman's reflective memoir proves well worth pondering as we confront the role reversals we ourselves will face—if we don't already."
    —*Newsday*

"A stunning memoir. Shulman is a brilliant and completely captivating writer."
—Harriet Lerner, Ph.D., author of *The Dance of Anger*

"Shulman's great theme has always been individual freedom. It is still her theme; it is still great. And now we watch as, with tender care and a good deal of sadness, she makes her theme a little more complicated, a little darker."
    —Paul Berman, author of *A Tale of Two Utopias: The Political Journey of the Generation of 1968*

"Profound, loving [and] universal."
    —*Pittsburgh Post-Gazette*

"As more of us live to unprecedented ages, inheriting our parents' care, may we do so with Alix's grace, insight, and good humor."
—Nancy Mairs, author of *Remembering the Bone House*

A Good Enough Daughter

Also by Alix Kates Shulman

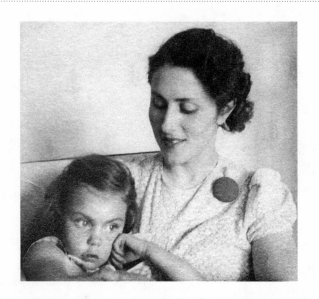

A Good Enough Daughter

A MEMOIR

Alix Kates Shulman

 SCHOCKEN BOOKS, NEW YORK

All rights reserved under International and Pan-American
Copyright Conventions. Published in the United States
by Schocken Books Inc., New York, and simultaneously
in Canada by Random House of Canada Limited, Toronto.
Distributed by Pantheon Books, a division of Random House,
Inc., New York. Originally published in hardcover in the
United States by Schocken Books Inc., New York, in 1999.

Schocken Books and colophon are registered trademarks of
Random House, Inc.

Grateful acknowledgment is made to Benny Davis Music
Company and Warner Bros. Publications U.S. Inc. for
permission to reprint and excerpt from "I'm Nobody's Baby"
by Benny Davis. Copyright © 1921, 1980 by Benny Davis
Music, EMI Feist Cat. Inc., and Warner Bros. Music. All
Rights Reserved. Reprinted by permission of Benny Davis
Music Company and Warner Bros. Publications U.S. Inc.,
Miami, FL 33014.

Library of Congress Cataloging-in-Publication Data
Shulman, Alix Kates.
A good enough daughter : a memoir / Alix Kates Shulman.
p.   cm.
ISBN 0-8052-1102-0
I. Shulman, Alix Kates—Biography.   2. Women authors,
American—20th century—Biography.   I. Title.
PS3569.H77Z474   1999   813'.54—dc21   [B]98-26159

Random House Web Address: *www.randomhouse.com*
Book design by Misha Beletsky
Printed in the United States of America
First Paperback Edition
9 8 7 6 5 4 3 2 1

Contents

Acknowledgments

For invaluable help, my thanks go to my tireless editor, Cecelia Cancellaro, my agent, Amanda Urban, and those friends and family members who informed or advised me: Eva Eisenberg, Laura Kates Feldman, Margaret Morganroth Gullette, Eugene Kates, Linda Trichter Metcalf, Nancy K. Miller, Honor Moore, Lynne Sharon Schwartz, Ann Snitow, Carol Stein, Lyn Thomas, Charlotte vanStolk, Susan Wittenberg, and Scott York. Finally, I am grateful to the Rockefeller Foundation and Gianna Celli for providing me with a serene month in residence at the Villa Serbelloni in Bellagio, Italy.

With my brother Bob,
in front of our Ashurst house, 1937

Preface

The books I've written tell me that my imagination sees the basic human drama as a struggle to slash patriarchal bonds—Part I: Take Off, Part II: Wise Up, Part III: Freedom. It's not just a feminist plot but an ancient imperative. Long before Simone de Beauvoir gave it a new significance, Jesus said it and Freud said it: *Leave thy father and thy mother.* Not trash or blame them, as is the fashion nowadays, but simply leave them. Not the bad parents only but the good ones too; it may even be harder to leave the good ones.

In their way, mine were the best of parents. Which is to say, they loved me abundantly, and when the time came for me to leave, which I did abruptly at twenty and seldom looked back, they let me go. Or to put it another way, they raised me to fly away but remained poised to catch me should I fall. I confess, this enabled me to take them shamelessly for granted once I took off—especially since I left my brother behind to clean up after me.

The lawyer who recently drew my will told me that in her experience, no matter what may have gone before, by the time parents reach their end, their children usually come through for them. Though, I've noticed, not always willingly. In my doctor's waiting room shortly after my parents died, I bumped into an old friend. "Last year I found out I have severe diabetes," she said. "Around the same time, my parents discovered they have it too. It's a terrible thing. All my life I struggled to escape from them, and after I finally got away, we're now connected again in this inseparable way." You always were, I wanted to say, but I held my tongue. Not till my parents were dead did I recognize escape as a leap on the long road home. My friend, whose parents were alive, would surely have bristled at my paradox.

I once read that in all literature there are only two plots: someone takes a journey or someone returns home. My other books have all recounted journeys. In this one I'm going home.

i | The Birthright

He took away my birthright; and behold, now he

has taken away my blessing.

— GENESIS

Bob, me, and two-year-old Johnny,
with Aunt Lil, the lawyer, on our front steps, 1939

Chapter 1

Whenever my parents came to visit me in New York City, I never met them at the airport; even during the years my husband had a car, I let them take a bus or taxi. Yet for forty years, each time I flew to Cleveland, my parents or brother met my plane no matter how I might demur. They did it out of courtesy and love and to ensure that no preventable discomfort could provide me an excuse to stay away. Still, once I wrenched myself out of their lives, nothing they did could bring me back till I was ready. The years rolled by, with some years only the occasional phone call and not one visit.

Now I was back—smack in the center of their lives. But this time my parents' car, armed with a car alarm, sat idle in its garage, and my brother Bob was dead. So I took an escalator down to the lowest level of the Cleveland airport, hopped on the convenient Rapid Transit that goes directly to downtown Cleveland and straight out Shaker Boulevard to a stop not two hundred feet from my parents' house. The Rapid had been whisking affluent professionals and businessmen from their downtown offices past Cleveland's industrial slums back up to their grand Shaker Heights houses ever since the 1920s, when the Van Sweringen brothers built the suburb, along with the fancy shops of Shaker Square, for successful Clevelanders—including the architect who built for himself my parents' house. I used to think the proximity of the house to the Rapid was Mom's trump in persuading Dad to sell the modest Cleveland-Heights-style three-bedroom on Ashurst Road where Bob and I grew up ("a postage stamp, but sweet," recalled my mother) for this six-bedroom English-style Shaker edifice: any day of the week he had only to step out the front door at five minutes past the hour or half hour to catch a train that would deposit him in a mere twelve minutes on Public Square, a five-minute walk from his office. Some people might have taken longer, lingering at the enticing windows of those great thriving department stores, Higbee's and May's, or (like me) stopping for cashews at the Nut House or for chocolates at Fannie Farmer; but S. S. Kates, born Samuel Simon and known around town as Speedy Sam, was in too much of a hurry to saunter. "I saw your dad on Prospect Avenue the other day walking so fast he leaned going around the corner," reported a young lawyer to me admiringly when my father was ninety. The brief memoir Dad composed at eighty-eight begins: "I was born in Cleveland, Ohio, November 10, 1901, in the kitchen of my parents' home, apparently in a rush to enter the world, and the habit of rushing—hurrying—being impatient—being early—has stayed with me ever since." Now I know my father agreed to buy the house for Mom for a weightier reason: Okay, Bummer, he said when the time came, I'll move if that will bring you back to me.

I carried my bags up the drive past the long leaf-strewn lawn spotted by one tall spruce and one towering elm. There used to be three elms, but two succumbed to Dutch elm disease years ago and were felled and hauled away.

Around the garage I trudged, past Mom's flower garden, dormant but for three late roses, to the back porch. Fishing out my key and the secret code to the alarm, I felt an illicit excitement: in the forty years my parents had lived in this house, I'd never stayed in it alone. Now I could search out its secrets without asking permission.

An ear-piercing wail violating the dignity of the entire stretch of boulevard shattered the air as I let myself in. Dropping my bags, I dashed past the kitchen to the foyer, flung open the door of the coat closet, and groped behind a scarf for a keypad to shut off the alarm. Consulting my notes, first I punched in the code for the outer ring, which controls doors, windows, cellar, and porch, then the one for the electric eyes that scan the interior spaces in search of an intruder who, breaking the beam, can set off a tremendous clanging in the house and simultaneously a signal at the police station.

This tyrannical burglar alarm (and its cousin in the car) was the highest-tech object in the house. Until a decade ago, my parents didn't own a clothes dryer, but had their laundry hung by wooden clothespins on lines strung the length of the basement. Though Mom was passionate about music and a lifelong concertgoer, they never upgraded their sound system to stereo, much less to cassettes or CDs, remaining content to play their old 33-rpm records on the same Magnavox phonograph on which I learned the classics back in the 1940s by playing them over and over endlessly, driving everyone away. (It was only fair, since Bob was allowed to blast through the air all summer long the play-by-play of every Cleveland Indians game.) Except for the garage-door opener and a microwave oven, there were no electronics in this house, no VCR or answering machine or even a digital clock, though my mother invested in an electric typewriter when she decided to write a novel at sixty-six. At eighty-two she considered buying a computer to write a book about Bob, but never did. I'd been using a computer for years by then, but I didn't encourage her. Worse, fearing her too old to learn, I was evasive when she sought my advice. Too bad—it might have kept her mind intact. That's one book I'd now give anything to read.

When the deafening noise stopped, I stretched a tentative toe into the hall before venturing out to the living room. Pale pleated drapes of beige linen covered the windows, dulling down the late afternoon light. I drew them open window by window as I circled the rooms—living room, sun porch, dining room, even the small corner library where my mother always sat with the drapes drawn tightly shut. Not that the neighbors could have seen her through the shrubbery, but for a public person Mom always husbanded her privacy, hugged close her secrets. Sunk into the cushions of the sofa with her stuffed datebook beside her and her mail piled on the low Japanese lacquered cabinet that held the telephone, she could linger all morning over coffee in negligee and slippers, the phone cradled on her shoulder, a pencil between her polished fingernails. A slow starter, compared to Speedy Sam. Or maybe just a leisurely dresser, given the rigors of her exacting toilette. Hurry up, Bummer, make it snappy—Dad's signature words to Mom, sixty years' worth of which are indelibly etched in my ears. He taps his foot and pulls out his pocket watch. Speed it up or we'll be late. Come on, move the bodouv!—short for *bodouviator,* Dad's elevated coinage for behind.

As light filled the library, I was taken aback to see no sign of life. The plants on the table drooped in their pots, the unanswered mail lay somewhere in a drawer, Mom's active datebook had taken its place in the cabinet alongside dead ones going back to the 1950s, the clock had stopped, and no smells wafted in from the kitchen.

Returning to the living room, where no book lay open on the coffee table, I walked to the farthest end to survey the vast expanse. So much space for just the two of them—as Bob repeatedly observed, bugging them to sell their house, forgetting that even back in 1954 when they bought it there were just the two of them. If you stood beside the Anthony Caro sculpture at one end, looking past the large tiled fireplace with Dad's Crystal Owl, bestowed by the American Arbitration Association for distinguished lifetime service, on the mantel, straight through the entrance hall, past the paneled dining room with its long mahogany table, marquetry sideboard, and tea cart with hammered silver tea service ("Your mother," pronounced their friend and neighbor, Carola de Florent, "set the most elegant table in all of Cleveland, down to the tiniest detail. The silver, the china, the table linens, every last teacup was exquisite. And the food!—the food was perfection!"), and on to the distant library, your eye took in an expanse of pale blue walls, blue carpet, and Persian rugs extending eighty feet from one end of the house to the other—and every table and wall boldly adorned with art. There they hung, my mother's pride, warranting the loud alarms: the de Kooning, the Motherwell, the Frankenthaler, the Avery, the Dubuffet, the two Stellas, the Kline, the Olitski, the Tworkov, the Nevelson— gay or serene, somber or wild, resplendent in their colors and forms, embodying my mother's ambition, resourcefulness, and taste, and, despite his ambivalent mix of disapproval and pride, my father's security and solace.

....

I plopped down on the living room couch to study the Nevelson while there was still light. A three-foot-square wooden construction of black-painted disks and cubes set inside an irregularly shaped black formica frame, it now belonged to me. Last year I asked for it—the only thing of value I ever asked for. Because it was the one piece in the collection I really loved, I said I hoped they would will it to me rather than leave to chance my drawing it in the elaborate face-off between my brother's children and me whereby, according to the wills, we were to take turns choosing what we wanted, so long as the values wound up equal. (Dad always made a fetish of equality between me and my brother, alive or per stirpes). We were finishing dinner at the time. Since she turned eighty, Mom had been gradually dispersing her things, at the end of each visit inviting her granddaughters to select a pair of antique cups from her collection and urging me to choose something valuable to take home; but I was so loath to appear acquisitive that I usually accepted only trifles. Tickled that at last I wanted something, Mom waved her fork and said, Well of course, darling, it's yours, and turning to my father asked, Why don't we give it to her now, Sam? Whereupon my father tossed his napkin on the table, leaped up, and penned a letter on the spot conveying the Nevelson to me. Signed, dated, witnessed, done.

Alone now in this empty house, too late I realized I should have admired her things more openly, accepted her gifts of love. After so many years apart it was foolish to feel that my independence could still be compromised or might melt away in love's heat. How old would we have to be before I would finally let down my guard?

Except for Milton Avery's *Purple Mountain Landscape*—another picture I admired and Mom's first major purchase for which in 1967, the very year I discovered the fledgling women's liberation movement, she scraped together a small down payment—the rest of the art was a blur to me, if not an outright embarrassment. Her collecting represented all I'd rejected when I fled Cleveland for New York at twenty: acquisitiveness, frivolity, suburban pretension. Not sharing her interest in art, I assumed the worst, unaware that at the same moment I was beginning to transform my life through feminism, my mother was opening a space in hers for her own suppressed ambitions. I remembered the chagrin I felt in the office of a SoHo gallery the day she bought the Tworkov. Show me what else you have, she said, prolonging the transaction while the normally imperious gallery owner offered coffee and fawned as he brought out canvas after canvas. My distress eventually drove me from the office into the gallery, where I pretended to look at pictures, then outside to wait. Yet Mom's shopping style on that day seemed hardly different from on those treasured days of my anointed childhood when we sat together on easy chairs in department store dress salons viewing garments displayed for us by a salesclerk who produced them one by one from a back room—a style that eventually drove my frugal father to wait outside, foot tapping, whenever Mom stepped into a store. In his later years he grew so phobic about shopping that when I took him with me to the wonderful farmers' market in New York's Union Square he wouldn't even sample the apple slices set out for tasting, afraid it might oblige us to buy. You go ahead, he'd say, I'll wait here.

Here was the very image of their conflict: she reaching out, he drawing in. And I? Torn between them, like him I left the gallery in disgust, like her I tasted every apple. Unable to endorse their differences, yet too implicated to make a choice, for a long time I simply fled them both.

....

In my childhood, extravagant love had flowed between us. Theirs were the trunks I scaled to see the world, theirs the fruit that nourished me, theirs the leafy canopy that sheltered me, theirs the sap that fed my curiosity. But they were firmly rooted in suburban Cleveland, a place I had come by the early 1950s to find so airless and constricting that I knew I would suffocate if I didn't leave. Which meant I would have to leave them too. But how—short of hacking myself off at the roots?

That brutal image matches the agonizing shock of my first return to my childhood house after leaving home at twenty: autumn chill, dead leaves massed along the porch steps as I open the door on the sudden smell of her perfume and the breath-stopping knowledge, like a blow to the solar plexus, of what I've thrown away in the name of freedom and can never regain. That ambitious lust for freedom that tempts each successive generation of Americans to obliterate its past propelled me in my rush toward independence to identify my family with everything I'd renounced—a move not only cruel but self-defeating, since my scorn was soaked in guilt. No wonder the first novel I attempted when I started to write in my thirties was about that family—a novel I abandoned after three chapters. I barely understood my own feelings, much less theirs. The independence I'd flaunted by leaving home was evidently still too shaky to support such scrutiny, and laying aside the manuscript, I took on other work, returning my parents to comforting oblivion.

*

In the big kitchen I rummaged around for a snack. Not much to choose from since I'd tossed out all the opened boxes preparing for my parents' move. A year earlier, after Dad fell from the stepladder trying to put away a bowl, I had cleaned out every cupboard and countertop. I'd weeded a rat's nest of yellowed recipes and clippings, tossed out a mountain of plastic bags, cleared the cluttered surfaces and rationalized the cupboards, moving the everyday dishes to the lower shelves and Mom's cup collection to the upper ones. Dad was grateful for my efforts, and even Mom, who had forbidden Dad to tackle the job, thanked me, though she soon complained that she could no longer find anything. Was it my zeal that confused her or her dementia? Gradually she'd been losing control of her things, letting objects stay wherever she dropped them in unattended piles that threatened to teeter into chaos unless my father or I rescued them.

I found an unopened box of raisins in a canister where I'd placed it during the grand cleanup. Always a staple in our house, raisins were Dad's choice egestion regulator, which he consumed daily to forestall constipation and once distributed to his children as performance rewards. One raisin for Number One, two raisins for Number Two; one to urinate, two to defecate. (These are the words our family used, no others. The rest Dad considered vulgar.) I remember the tenderness with which he held my small grubby hands in his big clean ones as I sat on my potty seat atop the toilet trying to let go, facing him perched on the bathtub rim hissing gently. After a while he turned on the sink faucet to add a trickle of water to his sibilant hiss and waited patiently while I concentrated. When at last my own trickle joined the chorus, I claimed my reward: a joyful grin spreading from his lips up his cheeks to his dancing blue eyes and the roots of his red hair—and a single raisin.

Still, Dad was deeply ambivalent about the body. Where

did innocence end and corruption begin? On the one hand, he crinkled his nose in embarrassed disgust at the etching Mom had hung in the study of a bathing nymph with exposed backside, which he disgruntledly dubbed *Pants Down;* on the other hand, our family showered together every weekend. On weekday mornings it was my joy to join my father in the downstairs lavatory, where he performed his daily ablutions in the nude—a pleasure abruptly replaced by shame the day he realized I was staring at his privates while he shaved his lathered chin. (How did he, focused intently on his beard, catch me looking? And why, after all those showers, did he care?) I was mortified by my breach, of which I was afterward daily reminded by the white towel invariably wrapped around his waist to hide those fascinating jiggling genitalia.

Yet my mother's jiggling parts as well as the dark beard of her pubis I was permitted to gaze upon unstintingly. Was it an instance of Mom's liberality triumphing over Dad's propriety, or simply a privilege of our mutual sex? Until I turned five, when Mom went to work for the WPA (Roosevelt's New Deal Works Progress Administration) and I began kindergarten, I daily accompanied her through her morning toilette—from the steamy shower where I sometimes joined her, to the cloud of lilac-scented talc she exuberantly applied with a giant puff to her body and my nose, to the womanly mysteries of her dressing. She was a small woman, only five feet two, but to me, a child—straight, tubular, skinny, hairless, not unlike my brother except in one particular—my mother was a marvel of strange undulating protuberances, a voluptuous creature of rippling flesh carefully hidden from the world inside an array of bizarre garments.

The complicated ritual of her dressing began with her

wriggling her way into a formidable elastic girdle stiff with stays, from which hung six garters. (No matter what she had planned for the day, never in those years did she skip that girdle.) She then plucked two silk stockings from her top dresser drawer, examined them for runs, and one at a time rolled them down to the ankle, inserted a narrow foot, and rolled them up her legs to attach to the garters above. As she had not put on underpants, her beard remained on tantalizing view beneath the girdle. Are my seams straight? she asked me, turning her back. Earnestly, I rendered my report, grateful to participate in those secret ceremonies. Next came the bra, which she hung from her shoulders and filled by bending over and lifting one breast at a time into the cups. Even at thirty her substantial breasts hung flat and low against her ribs—a result, she said, of the tight swaddling they'd undergone in the hospital to dry up her milk. Whatever they tell you, she warned me, don't do it, it breaks down all the tissues. Then came the panties, a satin slip, and finally the outfit she'd selected from the double rack of clothes on her side of the compact closet she shared with Dad. Sliding her dainty feet into leather pumps, she tied on a makeup cape and proceeded to do her hair, tweeze her eyebrows, and "put on her face" by applying the makeup promised to me as a distant reward for growing up.

Like Mom, I had no shame about my privates. We called them *maked* (two syllables), source of Number One, and *bodouviator* (five syllables), source of Number Two. Occasionally the formal *vagina,* comparable to Bob's *penis,* and the vernacular *behind,* but never *bum, rump, butt* or—heaven forbid!—*ass.*

To my decorous father words seemed to matter more than the natural parts and processes they represented. One of the rare times I saw his deliberate calm give way to rage was when, standing at the top of the stairs, I yelled Bull! down to my brother who was badmouthing me. Not *bull-shit,* just *bull:* in junior high school then, I didn't know what *bull* was short for. Dad took those stairs two at a time and, confronting me in the upstairs hall with his whole body tensed to shaking and his voice all but exploding from the strain of keeping it down near a whisper (never in my life did I hear him raise it in anger), said, Don't you ever let me hear you use that word again in this house! At the time, I laughed at him, regaling my friends with the story of his ludicrous linguistic purity, but secretly I was proud. This singular relationship to language, distinguishing him from all those fathers who cursed and hollered, became one of our strongest bonds, one of his golden gifts.

Though *maked* was possibly my own coinage, a noun variant of the common bathroom verb "to make," the latinate *bodouviator,* with its soupçon of French, was obviously Dad's. My very name, Alix, was another—the only one of his long string of hypothetical names Mom okayed. (Recently, I asked my parents what other names they'd considered, but all of them were buried deep in the imaginary realm where my father had found them.) Though odd, Alix had a sound basis: I was named after Alexander B. Cook, my father's mentor at law. Had I come out a boy, I would have been Alex; Dad decided that changing the *e* to *i* would adequately feminize it. How wrong he was! To my endless satisfaction, my name remained for me such an inextricable combination of the masculine and feminine that I grew up feeling secretly exempt from the standard restrictions of gender that limited everyone else. Indeed, until my first pregnancy erased all doubt, I secretly suspected I was really a male in an ambiguously female body—a suspicion confirmed each time I received mail addressed to *Mr.* Alix

Kates. As my body inevitably bound me to my mother, my name bound me to my father.

Jews, of course, were not supposed to name their children after anyone living—and Alexander B. Cook was not only alive but a little bit Christian, having agreed when he married to raise his son Catholic. Giving his child an invented name in honor of a living Catholic-Jew was a triumph of the optimism and rationality on which my father, self-made and proud of it, constructed his life. He had changed his own name from Katz to Kates soon after going into practice in 1925, when he discovered that there were already three lawyers in Cleveland named Samuel Katz. Katz itself had been a misrendering of Kotkess, the family name in Poland, Dad reported, lest we think he was trying to hide our Jewishness. Still, that duplicate-lawyer story doesn't explain why Dad also changed Katz to Kates for his parents and all his siblings but one, Louis, the oldest, who had already begun to make a name for himself as young Professor Katz of the medical faculty of Western Reserve University. Many children of immigrants aspired to make themselves over as pure Americans. My mother told me that her paternal family, in Russia named Radnitsky, had changed their name to Davis at Ellis Island on someone's shaky advice that most of the important people in America were named Davis. (Who? The Confederate president Jefferson Davis? The writers Rebecca Harding Davis and her son, Richard Harding Davis?) A cousin speculated that they were named for Grandpa's brother David, the first Radnitsky to immigrate. Mom's maternal family anglicized the German-sounding name Kurlander to Curtis during World War I to escape the rampant prejudice against all things German.

Words, names, heritage—none were immutable; all were opportunities for self-improvement. As a child, I practiced forging my parents' signatures until I had them by heart—not only for such practical purposes as writing school excuses but as a sign that with the magic of language, even written language, I could be my parents if it suited me. In America one could become anyone, just as my brother Bob, whom Mom and Dad legally adopted a year after his birth, became a Kates.

Dad's linguistic inventiveness and refinement of which I was so proud also ensured that as I grew toward my teens I would know precisely how to provoke him, eventually cultivating a foul mouth as a badge of independence. The single physical battle I ever had with my mother was over some now forgotten excremental expletive. The one-more-time-young-lady threshold had been crossed and the appropriate disciplinary sentence, thrice threatened and ultimately backed by the full force and credit of my father's authority, invoked—called in like an unpaid debt: Mom, teller at Dad's bank, must reluctantly wash out my mouth with soap. She dropped the handle of the carpet sweeper and grabbed a bar of Ivory—"99 and 44/100 percent pure," in stark contrast to my foul mouth. While one of her hands held me around the waist, the other searched my bobbing head for the erring mouth—the very one that had, just so, once blindly rooted for her nipple. But even as we struggled, leaving a soapy trail on the floor, we found the situation so farcical that soon we were doubled over laughing, tears streaking our cheeks like suds. Ivory—the very brand my mother had, with the extravagant generosity I treasured in her, permitted me to carve into fanciful animal shapes during the dark days of World War II when soap was strictly rationed.

Dad's verbal purity extended far beyond rejecting the "vulgar" and "profane." Semantic sloppiness, grammatical error, mispronunciation could equally distress him. A usage was correct or incorrect; in case of doubt, the dictionary could settle it. Although Mom had officially taught English, it was Dad who brought it into our house to party and dance, inviting the objective, subjunctive, and conditional to join us at dinner. You mean to *whom,* not to *who,* don't you? he would suggest gently; or, If I *were* you, not if I *was* you, since it's contrary to fact; or, I believe you mean it's *irritating,* or *exasperating,* not *aggravating,* sweetheart: a feeling may be aggravated but aggravated is not a feeling. As Dad's first mentor—the chief engineer of General Electric, who hired Dad fresh out of high school as his stenographer— urged him to stretch his vocabulary and soften his guttural *ng*-ending words, so Dad attempted to improve us. Gently now, children, softly, try to modulate your voices, was his usual response to our arguments. Speak up, son. Don't mumble. Try to e-nun-ci-ate, he was always bugging Bob, who supplemented his thumb sucking and nail biting by chewing his syllables and swallowing his vowels.

Though Bob resented Dad's corrections of our speech, I welcomed them. If English was the mystery train that had carried him out of poverty into the law and onto the Heights, I didn't want to miss it. Like him, I tried for ten new words a day and several books a week, though I stopped short of reciting famous speeches before the mirror.

*

When evening fell, I turned on the lights and took my bags upstairs. The wide, graceful staircase had been significantly narrowed by a chairlift I'd had installed a year ago (the Electric Chair, Dad called it), following Dad's hospital stay. Several of the signed prints that lined the stairway had to be moved to make room, but the Picasso, the Matisse, and the

Rockwell Kent were still there. More art in the upstairs hall and in every bedroom: constructions, drawings, muscular prints, and, leaning against a file cabinet in Mom's dressing room/studio, the tall framed oil painting she bought in Paris that a curator from the Cleveland Museum suggested might be a genuine Maurice Prendergast. What a flurry of research followed! Imagine! said Dad, eyes widening like shining moons. It might turn out to be worth a tremendous sum of money. Can you beat that?

Was it a Prendergast? Until that moment I'd neither known nor cared, preferring to remain aloof from Mom's collecting; but as the trustee of her estate, soon I'd have to find out. And after the art, the antiques. And the fine china, silver, linens, jewelry. And the books, thousands of them, filling the bookshelves and piled on every radiator and in cartons in the attic—books on history, law, biography, belles lettres, plus a whole library of Mom's French books, and art books on every artist who ever caught her eye.

Now all this must be sold. My parents have moved halfway downtown to a pair of rooms in the Judson Park Retirement Community, and I have returned to discharge my filial duty to see them through to the end.

Chapter 2

It felt more like a beginning than an end, like the exhilarating adventure of launching a new book. I did not take in that my parents would die. Someday, of course—but that day seemed no closer than it ever had, hardly closer than my own death. My grandmother had lived to be a hundred; why not they? True, at ninety-three Dad's heart was failing and at eighty-seven Mom's memory was shot; each had recently suffered a hospital siege. But to me, heir to my parents' midwestern optimism and temperamentally committed to the dictum "Never too late!" death seemed distant, alien, unthinkable.

I ought to have known better. For several years they had both been dramatically declining. Mom's slide had begun with my brother's death in 1989, which plunged her into despair. She was eighty-two, he fifty-seven. One week she was charming my New York friends at my third wedding with a throaty rendition in English of Marlene Dietrich's signature song, "Falling in Love Again," and the next she withdrew to bed in her darkened room.

Then, weeks after she emerged from her year of mourning, she announced she was going to write a memoir about Bob. Dad had written his own personal reminiscences in the months following Bob's death: thirty pages of anecdote that he sent around to the family with a cover letter stating: "Once, in high school, I was good enough in my typing class to win a gold medal. But that was a long time ago, and as the enclosure demonstrates, my typing skill has greatly diminished. No doubt there are errors and omissions in the story. There are also deliberate omissions of an intimate nature." But Mom never started hers.

Gradually, Dad took over the cooking and household management until, by the time he retired completely at age ninety, he was doing every chore except the heavy cleaning. For that, two efficient women who owned a cleaning service arrived with equipment every second Tuesday and, like a double helix ensuring order, whirled down from the top, scouring and sweeping, while Mom and Dad sat quietly in the living room waiting for them to finish. Months after Dad's gala ninetieth birthday party, to which I flew from my teaching post in Hawaii carrying fresh jasmine leis for the stars, their physician, Dr. Murphy, began urging them to hire live-in help.

Nonsense! We can manage by ourselves, they insisted. Instead, they gave a small dinner party for their most trusted friends and neighbors, handing out with the after-dinner drinks the secret code of their burglar alarm and the phone numbers of their doctors and nearest relatives, in case of emergency. Once or twice a week Dad continued to take the Rapid downtown to his office, the bank, and the public library, where he exchanged six old books for six new ones. "Beginning as a young boy," he wrote in his memoir, "I frequented the public library near my home. I started by devouring all the fairy tales I could find, and then Aesop's Fables, stories of the knights of King Arthur's round table, and of the Greek, Roman, and Scandinavian gods. I later read and still read widely in biography, history, and literature in general." Now in his old age, for the first time in his life, he indulged himself in popular novels, adventure tales, and mysteries in place of more edifying works. "What the hell," he said to me, grinning with freedom.

But the freedom was short-lived. Soon Dad began to fall and Mom to forget. Having neglected to wear his galoshes, at ninety-one he fell on the ice in front of the barbershop; at ninety-two he fell from a ladder in the kitchen as he was changing a lightbulb, and later slipped in the bathtub. He was often covered with bruises. Too late I had handholds installed in each shower and laid rubber mats in the tubs. As for Mom, in a single phone conversation she could repeat the same question half a dozen times, forgetting the answer of a moment before. She forgot to take her pills. Always a demon driver, she forgot the route to the dry cleaner, the hairdresser. By default Dad, whom she'd forbidden to drive after dusk because of his poor night vision, began chauffeuring her to all her appointments until she stopped going. Hey, Bummer, don't you need to have your hair done? It's Thursday, said Dad. I'll get to it when I'm ready, she replied.

I began to phone them every Sunday for their news. In preparation for winter, dreading another of Dad's falls, I had iron railings installed alongside the front and back exterior stairs and while I was at it a mahogany banister for the graceful interior staircase down which Mom had made her famous entrances to her parties after all her guests had assembled. (Most people assumed those belated entrances were calculated for dramatic effect, but her intimates knew they resulted from pokiness, not showmanship.) In small ways I tried to ease their daily lives. I found a supermarket that took phone orders and delivered. After Dad vacated his office, I convinced him to bank at a nearby branch and patronize the local public library instead of riding all the way downtown. To spare him the relentless preparation of every meal, I begged him to allow me to hire help and, when he refused, suggested ordering in some of their meals, which he huffily dismissed. Soon I stepped up my phone calls from once a week to every other day.

By the following year, they'd both had bouts in the hospital—she with the first of a series of intestinal infections (diverticulitis), he with congestive heart failure. Sitting up in the hospital bed, he said, half amused, half sheepish, "They say it's because of an overdose of salt in the corned-beef sandwich with mustard and two dill pickles I had for lunch. Can you beat that?" Each time, I flew to Cleveland and stayed until they were back home and settled. But daily care for them was urgent. That winter, the furnace conked out twice, the automatic garage door stopped working, the car needed another inspection. I wondered how they'd manage to handle it all, and Dad had no answers. A cardiology resident in the hospital informed him that with his heart so weak he probably had only another year to live. "Frankly, I'm ready to die right now," he confided to me, "but your mother needs me."

Before the doctor's news my parents had permitted me to begin looking for an apartment where there'd be no stairs to negotiate or maintenance problems. But learning he had only a year to live, Dad changed his mind, preferring not to spend his remaining time—he was pushing ninety-three—on real estate and packing. (How different from Mom who, given a year to live at fifty-two, wrote in an essay, "While out loud and even to myself off the top of my head I readily admitted that I had only an ever diminishing year to live, deep inside myself I knew I was fighting that verdict with all my being. I *would* be well. I was determined. I thought often of that 5% chance of remission. Why not me? In my

inner self I commanded the malignant cells to go away.")
Instead of calling realtors, I had the chairlift installed and,
invoking doctor's orders, hired a nine-to-five caregiver.
Then I laid in a store of low-salt soups and saltless season-
ings and wrote out half a dozen simple low-salt recipes.

Just home from the hospital, too weak to raise himself
from the bathtub, at first Dad refused my help, preferring
to remain in the tub. "Please, Daddy, I promise I won't
look. Just let me help lift you up." As I lifted his frail bones,
he felt as light as a child, but his groans carried the weight of
a century. After that he gave up his cherished daily baths for
weekly showers.

Dr. Murphy stepped up his campaign to get them to
move to a retirement home. "Sam, you are too weak to take
care of Dorothy, and she's going to get harder and harder to
manage. Look—you might as well know it—Dorothy's in
the early stages of Alzheimer's disease."

Alzheimer's disease! Just because she repeated herself,
lost her way, and wouldn't take her pills? We refused to believe it. "She's just being stubborn," said Dad, and after futilely trying myself to get her to take her medications, I
agreed. "What's the problem, Mom? Just open your mouth
and pop it in—what's the matter with you?" Despite her
uncharacteristic recalcitrance, I thought the doctor, an on-
cologist, had overstepped his expertise.

After that I phoned them every day, visited every month
or two and in each new emergency. On the doctor's urging,
my husband and I surveyed the Cleveland retirement
homes. The horror of the worst sent us reeling to the best
till we narrowed the choice to two. Dad was torn but coop-
erative as he filled out the applications. "Gee, Al," he said,
shaking his head, "moving out of this house is going to be
one hell of a job."

"Don't worry, I'll handle it," I promised—though I had no idea how.

Traditional Judson Park seemed the most flexible home, with its three different care levels: Independent Living, Assisted Living, and Nursing, the latter with its own three graduated levels of care. It ran regular excursions by van to the art museum, the symphony, the supermarket. There was a well-stocked library, a beauty parlor, a barbershop, an auditorium, a greenhouse for the amateur gardeners, physical therapy rooms, a commissary, a bank—everything my parents might need. It would be easy for me to reach by Rapid from the airport after the car was sold, and the hospital was only five minutes away. On the other hand, perhaps they would feel more comfortable at the newly built Jewish Montefiore Home in suburban Beachwood. I tried to involve Dad in the selection process, but he refused even to visit the homes until required. "I leave it to you," he said, taking an active interest only in the costs. When we finally sat down with the numbers, he satisfied himself that by renting an apartment in Independent Living, with only Mom receiving assistance, and by prudently investing the proceeds from the sale of their house and art supplemented by Social Security, the cost would be manageable. Interviews were scheduled.

Then in the middle of one night Mom collapsed, vomiting and in pain, and all plans went on hold. The intestinal infection was treatable with antibiotics, but since she couldn't keep anything down, she had to receive the medication intravenously—which meant the hospital.

As we sat in her hospital room gossiping together, I put off imagining the future. Aside from her appalling forgetfulness, Mom was her familiar vivacious self as she and Dad, to amuse my husband, performed what we'd come to call the Sam and Dorothy Act, Dad playing straight man to Mom's playful vamp. Returning to Mom's room from a fast lunch in the hospital cafeteria, Dad discovered a rabbi's card on her nightstand. With a frown of anticlerical indignation he tore it into small pieces. An hour later the rabbi popped his head through the open door and said, "I see you have visitors, Mrs. Kates, so I won't stay now. But you can call me if you need me, you have my card." Dad and I exchanged a smile. As soon as the rabbi was gone, Dad said, "These goldarned chaplains should wait till they're called." But Mom countered perkily, "I don't know—this one's a rather sweet rabbi." The next morning when we arrived, Mom was sitting up in bed looking fresh. Dad kissed the top of her head and said, "You're looking and smelling lovely this morning, Bummer. Did you shampoo your hair?" Mom said, "A nice young man, Patrick, shampooed me. Not just my hair but my whole body. He gave me such a nice shower." Every few minutes she repeated the remark until finally Dad rose to the bait and said, "You let a young man wash you?" "Why not?" said Mom. "Patrick is such a nice young man. Why shouldn't I let him wash me?"

From time to time she grabbed her head and moaned in pain. But she refused all pills, even pain pills, and when a nurse who wasn't Patrick began insisting, she became angry and announced she was going home. "Get my clothes, Alix," she said, "I'm not staying here another minute."

We could not placate her.

"I will not be kept prisoner. Sam," she ordered, "get the car. Alix, please come here and help me find my shoes."

Seeing there was nothing to be done, Dr. Murphy loaded us with prescriptions and ordered her release, but not before taking us aside to deliver an urgent warning: "Right now Dorothy's still borderline. But if she gets much worse, she won't be able to qualify for Assisted Living. If you want to stay together, Sam, you'll have to arrange the interviews quickly and be admitted very soon. You simply cannot go on trying to care for her yourself without adequate help. You are both at risk."

Indeed, even with round-the-clock practical nurses attending her at home, Mom was getting to be too much for Dad. She lay in bed in her book-lined room with the shades drawn, moaning in pain, unable to eat, unable to move her bowels. "Ooh, ooh, ooh, ooh," was her mantra. It seemed connected with her muscles: whenever she tried to stand or take a step, she repeated her rhythmic "Ooh, ooh, ooh, ooh."

"Could you try not to make that noise, Mom," I urged, thinking of the upcoming interviews.

"I know. It's just an ugly habit," she said. But as she inched toward the bathroom on her swollen feet, leaning on Dad's arm, there it was again, "Ooh, ooh, ooh, ooh," with each step. She refused the cane I bought her, would not take her pills. Dad insisted on sleeping in her bed though she was up and down all night trying to move her bowels, failing, moaning. Laxatives might have helped but she continued to refuse all medications even though the caregivers (one for days, one for nights) tried to slip them to her in her orange juice, as Dr. Murphy advised. She wasn't buying it. As I tried to administer the suppositories he prescribed, she screamed in terror. Finally, Dr. Murphy had to clean her out by hand, reaching his plastic-gloved fingers high up inside her as she screamed. Her once elegant room looked and smelled like a hospital, with a bedside potty, a plastic-covered path to the bathroom, a shelfful of pills, absorbent pads on the sheets. Never again would she sit at her dressing table gazing into the three-paneled French mirror before which she'd spent untold hours applying scented lotions, restorative unguents, expensive cosmetics and perfumes. She refused to brush her teeth, no longer bothered to dress, and seldom went downstairs.

To rout chaos with order and preserve a semblance of decorum, Dad pursued his lifelong habits. Early each morning he returned to his room to wash, shave, and dress, then rode his chairlift down to the kitchen where he warmed his milk, poured himself a bowl of cereal, peeled an orange, toasted two slices of bread, and brought in the newspaper. Fortified with food and news, he rode back upstairs to Mom carrying a glass of fresh orange juice to begin the day's increasingly futile struggle to get her to please, Bummer, just open your mouth and swallow this one tiny pill.

Slowly she recovered enough to receive the interviewers. She charmed them with coffee and cakes served in that long, stately, art-adorned living room. Her composure was so habitual that she almost got away with her faked responses to the interview questions: "Yes, perhaps, but on the other hand . . . what do you think, Sam—do you think Clinton is still the president?"

I was elated when they were provisionally admitted to Judson for a two-to-six-week trial. I packed them each a suitcase and helped them move to a furnished suite on the Assisted Living floor. Breakfasts were delivered to their suite, Dad prepared their lunches, and they took their dinners in the elegant Fisher Dining Room with its fresh flowers on every table, crisp linen tablecloths, varied menus, attentive waiters, and sprinkling of familiar faces from their past. Mom's medications were administered by a nurse, and she was given biweekly baths by an aide who also helped her to dress. No more snow and ice for Dad to negotiate, no lightbulbs to change, no furnace or car to worry about, no undetected falls to risk. Knowing that every night someone checked to see that all the residents were safely in their rooms, I heaved a sigh of relief and gladly resumed my free and separate life.

*

In the middle bedroom where I usually slept, I opened my bags and shook out what needed shaking. But when I tried to hang up my clothes, I found the closet so stuffed with my mother's that there was hardly room for mine. The closets of every bedroom but Dad's were packed with a jumble of dresses, suits, and outfits too good to throw away. (I confess that though my clothes are quite ordinary my own closet too is full.) Every corner of the house was so brimming with treasures that despite my ostentatious antithing obsession I never tired of delving into cupboards and drawers whenever I came back to visit. In the linen room were bedsheets and towels in use since my childhood. In the cellar was the mangle Mom used to press our sheets in the 1940s (I still have a scar where I burned myself), the workbench piled with tools my bookish father seldom used, canceled checks going back to the 1920s, and even the industrial scale used by Grandpa Davis to weigh the scrap metal from which he tried to eke out a living during the Depression. In one bedroom was a dresser drawer full of photographs, in another a tall file cabinet stuffed with Mom's papers, and in Dad's top bureau drawer a box of brittle documents tied with ancient ribbon. I could hardly wait to begin trawling for secrets, like a child loose again in Grandma's attic or back in my old treasure-hunting dream, but I still had to hang up my clothes.

To make room I began pulling from the closet outfits so dated or timeless that over the years they became a private bond between my mother and her visiting granddaughters, Lisa and Amy, who sometimes put on dress-up shows for her, trying to decide which garments to take back home. I could see I'd have to get them to Cleveland one last time to claim what they wanted before everything went. And their brothers, too, Adam and Steve, if there was anything to interest single men in their thirties oblivious of fashion and the past.

I checked my father's room to see. Dad's closet was the opposite of Mom's—everything in perfect order. Hanging on wooden hangers were his three-piece suits and jackets, arranged by season. Ties hung on tie racks, belts on belt racks. A jumbo shoeshine kit, which Dad used every week of his adult life until he moved to Judson, took up a whole shelf. Polished shoes, each straining under its own arched shoetree, were tucked into built-in mahogany drawers. The bottom drawer was padlocked shut, allowing me to hope that should I find the key the treasure inside might please a grandson.

Dad, unlike Mom, seldom bought a new item if an old one would do and quickly disposed of things he no longer deemed useful. Sometimes he overdid this tendency. When he finally vacated his office at ninety-two, I caught him just as he was about to jettison his collection of four thousand arbitration decisions and as many case files.

Daddy, don't!

Why not?

Because they are valuable documents of labor history.

Nonsense, he replied with self-deprecating modesty, there are thousands of decisions like these in the record. Mine are of no special interest to anyone. And I'm ready to clear out of this office.

Many years before, in a zealous cleanup I had myself

tossed out dozens of stories Dad had penned on yellow legal pads and mailed to his New York grandchildren every few weeks. Once my children had outgrown those "Grandpa Sam stories"—sentimental parables about wounded birds and loyal dogs, with predictably uplifting endings—I saw no need to keep them. But when Dad hinted, after my own books for children began to be published, that perhaps a collection of his stories might also find an outside audience, I was evasive and chagrined. Eager to avoid a repeat of that mistake, I begged him to give me two weeks to find a home for the decisions before he threw them out. He reluctantly agreed. In the end, the chief archivist of the Ohio Historical Society personally drove up from Columbus to get the papers—which now reside in the Samuel S. Kates Collection, along with other documents and photos I rescued: a monument to Dad's judiciousness and my belated filial fortitude.

At Dad's dresser I stopped before the hinged double picture frame that, like a cross before a vampire, kept my mother from entering this room for years after Bob died. She couldn't bear to see Bob's handsome face looking out from one-half of the frame, despite mine laughing in the other half. The two portraits, which sat on this dresser for years, were taken when we were each in our mid-forties. In mine I am gleeful with the pleasure of having just completed my second novel; in Bob's, the corners of his mouth turn ever so slightly upward hinting at a smile—one of the few smiles I remember him bestowing on a camera. Even from inside our separate frames we look away from each other, failing to connect. Or, worse, connecting inversely: if Bob is frowning, I'm sure to be smiling, and if Bob is about to smile, as he is here, you can bet I'll have just broken into a full-throated laugh. That's how it was between us, to the very end, and our parents could do nothing about it.

Chapter 3

My brother Bob. Firstborn. Male. My parents' child before I arrived. He should have had the birthright. But he lost it soon after birth and got charity instead. Like a winning lottery ticket that expires if you fail to claim your winnings, a birthright is an empty thing unless it is collected. Bob's first one expired a week after his birth, when his mother died of childbed fever in rural Pennsylvania while his bewildered father, my mother's oldest brother, Louis, stood by watching helplessly. His second one expired when I was born.

We called his father Papadear instead of Uncle Louis to distinguish him from our other Uncle Louis, Dad's brother, Dr. Louis Katz. Papadear was a whiskey-drinking gambling man with a gravelly voice who wore his fedora pushed back on his head like movie tough guys of that era. He made a meager living selling used-car parts from the yard of his tumbledown house, which was clovered with rusty heaps, old tires, used motor parts. When his wife died suddenly, he lacked the funds or will to raise their children on his own. Few men considered keeping their motherless children in 1931, that high Depression year when Bob was born; a motherless child was an orphan. Papadear's children were headed for Belfaire, Cleveland's Jewish orphanage, until my parents agreed to take the newborn Bob, and our grandparents, who had already raised seven children of their own, took six-year-old Marian.

My parents took Bob home to Cleveland and moved him into the extra room conditionally planned for me. He got the room, but when I was born eleven months after him, I joined him in the room and took the birthright.

Why? Like me, Bob was half Davis—he had Mom's strong Davis chin, straight nose, slender nostrils, deep-set brown eyes, and the thick brown hair of all the Davis men, destined to begin falling out in middle age. But no part of him was Kates—a handicap in Daddy's eyes. Had our parents never had another child, Bob would have kept the birthright. But as the one true Kates, I got it.

Here was something new: a girl, a secondborn, with a boy's name and the birthright. Fertile soil in which to grow a future feminist. That my advantage sprang from Bob's loss was the unspoken price. Of course, every child gets displaced by the younger sibling, but I displaced Bob doubly by being our parents' natural child, while he was merely adopted.

No, *merely* won't do. *Momentously* is more like it. Though it was rarely referred to in our house, Bob's adoption was a central fact of our childhood—not only his but mine. Not that his misfortune was my fault, but it was the fortuitous source of my guilty privilege, which always lurked beneath the surface of our lives. The more our parents tried to undo it, the more power it had over us. The mere mention of Bob's natural mother (whom we called Henrietta but I secretly thought of as his "real" mother), or a visit from his other sister, my cousin Marian, or from Papadear, or an allusion to the loaded word *adopted* reminded me instantly of Bob's tragedy and my luck.

When school friends asked me in lowered voices if it was true that Bob was adopted, I hid my guilt in a wash of loyalty. Though it was technically true, I explained with an air of noblesse oblige, in fact Bob was our parents' child before I was even born—as if such priority could insure his rights and render us a normal family. Pressed further, I tried to balance Bob's loss of a mother against the privilege of having two fathers, one of whom had the charming name of Papadear. But this defense was disingenuous because despite that endearing name, which lent Papadear a certain pizzazz, there was scant comfort in a father who for reasons never adequately explained willingly gave away his children. He barely knew how to speak to us. On his rare visits from Pennsylvania to Cleveland, he seemed as embarrassed as we by the filial complications that had Marian calling him Daddy even as Bob called him Papadear, reserving "Daddy" for my father. Bob always smiled shyly at Papadear, like a blushing wallflower being asked to dance. What, I often wondered, did he feel. Ostensibly, with two families he was twice as rich as I was—a view subtly promoted in our house. From another angle, abandoned by his real parents he was infinitely poorer: thumb sucker, nail biter, mumbler, whiner, tattletale, orphan.

Recently, Marian told me that she was born in a hospital, but when Bob was born six years later in the gloom of the Depression, they barely had enough money for food, much less a hospital. "That's why my mother died," she said. Her mother tried to weave baskets out of reeds to earn some cash, but when Papadear got any money, he would drink and gamble it away. "He was really bad. He was terrible to my mother. Even when we had no food on the table, he'd go off into the woods to drink and gamble with his cronies. Sometimes my mother would send me out to bring him home. I hadn't learned how to tell time yet, but she'd give me her watch to take, saying, 'When the big hand gets here, you start acting bad. Then he'll have to bring you home.' " After Bob's birth Henrietta's fever reached 109 degrees. Marian was not allowed into her mother's room. "I went up and looked at the new baby, though. He was all red, and I told my father they should give him back." Henrietta came from a poor Pittsburgh family. Marian saw them regularly all her life. But they refused to see Bob because they held him responsible for Henrietta's death.

After my parents took in Bob, Marian was slated to go to Belfaire. But at the last minute Grandma, unwilling to condemn a Davis to an orphanage, agreed to keep her. "Back then we were so poor," Marian told me, "that I wouldn't have been able to ride the streetcar to school if Aunt Dorothy—your mother—hadn't given me the money for my streetcar pass. Sure, I sometimes used my pass to take you and Bob to the movies or the public pool, but that was just Aunt Dorothy's excuse to give me money. My father sent us a little now and then, and so did the others—Uncle Harry sent Grandma a check every month. But your mother was always specially good to me. She gave me money, and she bought me clothes and my first bicycle. I never understood why Bob was so bossy to your parents. He seemed so much better off than I was."

I never pitied Marian—probably because she was enviably older and independent: she made her own clothes, dated soldiers on the sly, and before I left grade school joined the Marines. But Bob was another story.

Now I wonder why we, like other siblings, could not have had equal birthrights. Our parents certainly acted as if we did; yet both of us sensed my singular advantage. Since our parents vehemently denied its existence we could never get to the bottom of it or know its source. Bob believed I maintained it unfairly through sly manipulations and precocity; I chalked it up to his alien origins. For this reason, it was with tinges of pity and guilt, as well as the common resentment and rage, that I pressed my advantage in our struggles. Bob scorned my pity. What he wanted was justice, which he sometimes triumphantly took into his own hands.

Too bad the daily gift of Bob's lucky rescue didn't outweigh for me his primal loss. Too bad our open acknowledgment of his adoption didn't rout the embarrassment and guilt that cloaked all family irregularities in that tight unyielding society, where even divorce was so shameful that one friend claimed her father had died at Pearl Harbor rather than admit her parents were divorced. However ordinary Bob's life may have been to him, to me it was both proof of my privilege and the embodiment of my peril. With his plight filling the air like noise, I feared I'd someday have to pay through a comparable loss of my own. Maybe that's why I had to get away.

One of Bob's hands is holding my neck, the other is tilting my chin as he plants a kiss below my lips, like kisses in movie close-ups—though in 1935, when this picture was taken, I doubt we'd been to the movies. Bob is just shy of four, I of three: I recognize the clothes. He's wearing his brown high-top shoes over dark kneesocks, rimmed by a wide contrasting stripe, and short pants beneath his double-breasted tweed coat. I'm in white anklets and white lace-up shoes, polished, I'm sure, that very day by Dad before we set off for our Davis grandparents' house on Kempton Road, where this picture is being snapped; my thighs are bare beneath my spring coat which, though the photo is black and white, I know is blue wool, satin lined, and soft to the touch. My eyes are closed, my right leg is blurred with pivotal motion: I'm trying to get away. Stand still now, hold it one more sec, kiss her, Bobby, go on, kiss her! cries Dad, one eye squinting, one on the camera—and snaps the picture before I can break free.

*

With only eleven months between us, until we started school my brother and I were a unit: Alix-and-Bobby, as inseparable a pair as the mythical Alice-and-Jerry we would encounter in the first-grade readers. Still, my first vivid memory begins alone, age three, my brother nowhere in sight, as I wake swimming in pain from an ether swoon to see through the bars of my hospital crib a pair of dark tonsils floating in a jar on my bedside table. Fearsome marvel of nature!—not only that two distinct parts of me had been snipped from my dark interior while I slept but that they were such large, bloody, protoplasmic parts.

This shocking experience, together with the blue-black jolt I received as I sat on the floor sticking a hairpin into an electric outlet; and the excruciating bee sting that jerked me screaming to my feet from the top step of the back stairs where I'd been sitting alone minding my own business, an affront so unexpected and insulting as to leave me nature-shy; and, worst of all, my inconsolable grief when my mother, despite repeated promises, confessed that my small cast-iron turkey, which had fallen from a shelf and snapped in two, couldn't be mended after all—these scenes confirm that our most vivid early memories coalesce around helplessness and pain. As Sally Belfrage writes in her memoir, "Happy memories are all alike—they fade into a pleasant blur; miserable memories stay distinct forever. Maybe that's why so many people claim to have had an awful childhood, while the actual children that you see look generally content enough . . . yet all the while, they are collecting evidence for what will turn into their *bitter past,* gathering recollections that will cling to them like burrs."

Back home from the hospital in the room I shared with Bob in the rented side-by-side on Woodmere Road, I had my first taste of a stardom I didn't have to share. A stream of visitors brought a stream of gifts, and Aunt Jeannette, radio's Singing Lady, dedicated a song to me on the air. My other memories of that house where we lived till I was four have Bob in them: Bob free in a big chair while I'm locked in a high chair; Bob pushing my bouncer; Bob descending the steep stairs to the outside door while I watch from the fern-filled sun parlor. Then at last I bump slowly down the stairs on my bodouviator; next I learn to take them upright one at a time, pausing on each; then, left foot on one step, right on the next, carefully I hold the banister or my mother's hand; finally, flexing my knees, I dash after Bob out the door into the world.

Hand in hand we ventured around that great block fronting four entirely different streets—ours to explore as long as we never stepped off a curb. Clockwise we traveled along the slate sidewalk, between tree lawns on our left and houses on our right, around the corner to Colchester, where the Klappers, fellow members with our parents of the Pisha Pasha Club, promised sweets if we made it to their door—a daunting journey that made us brave. Though we were only three and four, in a show of trust our parents let us go—as they let each of us at the age of five go alone on a train to visit our Pittsburgh aunts and uncles.

My memories of that weekend never fade—from the moment Mom labeled me front and back and, with the admonition that I not talk to strange men, handed me into the charge of a conductor, until I returned four days later bursting with stories. I can still feel my nose and palms pressed against the cold train window as my family, in feathered hat, fedora, and cap, are suddenly replaced by tunnels, hills, and towns; still perfectly recall Aunt Rosemary's nervous giggle of surprise at finding me playing rummy with a dark-haired man I'd picked up in the dining car (so much for parental admonitions!) when she came on board to collect me one stop before my destination; can feel the wind in my hair as, seated between my aunt and uncle in their open roadster, we tool through the Allegheny hills; still see my glamorous relatives in their sartorial splendor at the Rayart Studios, their commercial art company where they worked in a downtown skyscraper: Uncle Ray in his famous spats, Uncle Harry with diamond tie tack, Aunt Rita and chic Aunt Rosemary in the smart veiled hats and matching gloves they seemed never to remove. Then the great moment: Uncle Ray takes my hand and asks, How would you like a wristwatch, little niece? He leads me into a large room where half a dozen men in shirtsleeves and green eyeshades stand before drawing boards. One of them paints on my wrist a perfect watch with a red-and-yellow strap, a silver buckle, and the hands of the face pointing ever to ten-fifteen. The next day on the lawn of their grand house in Brookside Farms, Uncle Ray sets me on the back of their Great Dane, Dan, whose shoulders come up to mine, places my hands around Dan's muscular neck, and sends us galloping across the lawn, while he and my aunt, sipping cocktails, watch from lawn chairs. Well done, little jockey! cries Uncle Ray, lifting me to the ground. Aunt Rosemary pours orange juice for me into a long-stemmed cocktail glass just like theirs.

Sending a five-year-old alone on a long train ride would today be considered criminal neglect; still, that solo journey was a high point of my childhood that lodged in my imagination to lure me toward adventure and away.

In his later years Dad, committed to the bright side, liked to remind me that back in our childhood Bob was my protector, who once, though terrified himself, interposed his body between me and a menacing dog. I don't remember that. What I remember is stepping out and roaming free.

*

In time for me to begin kindergarten and Bob first grade at Canterbury Elementary School, we moved from the Woodmere Road side-by-side to a single-family house on Ashurst Road. Mom traded her indoor ferns for an outdoor garden where each spring lilies of the valley, those delicate flowers scaled to a small child's hand, grew amid a border of blue myrtle. Dad traded rent, which he considered wasteful, for equity. And Bob and I each got a room of our own.

Over and over, I drew that house, from the age of four until I left it at twenty—first with pencil, then crayons, then charcoal, then watercolors—but I couldn't get to the bottom of it, couldn't see why Mom needed to leave it. It had a living-dining room, kitchen, lavatory, and tiny study on the first floor, three bedrooms and a bath on the second, and a slant-ceilinged room and bath with an old-fashioned claw-footed tub on the third. The long narrow living room, painted turquoise blue, held Mom's baby grand piano at one end and a folded drop-leaf table at the other. It would have been more efficient to keep the table always open instead of rolling it out each night at dinnertime, but Mom wanted the feeling of space. Bob's room was papered in a "masculine" brown-and-beige plaid, and my room—called the nursery, though my crib had gone directly to the third floor—in a pattern I selected: a blue-and-pink sky teeming with children swinging on stars and crescent moons. I was both stimulated and soothed as I lay in my grown-up bed studying the pattern's variations and repeats, filling my last waking moments with every combination of child, sky, star, and moon.

If I saw that paper now, I'd surely be embarrased by my conventional taste. Little wonder that the next time my room was decorated, when I was in high school, I made my antisentimental statement with stark brown walls. But in memory it's the nursery I prize—still as vivid and enchanting as the children's books I treasure or my mother's lullabies.

Outside, a sloping front lawn with two birch trees tall enough to enable me to earn the nickname "Climbing Kates" led to a three-step stoop. In picture after picture Bob and I sit on the top step looking at the camera. Sometimes someone else is in the picture—our mother in a negligee with her arms around us, or one of our visiting aunts. But usually it's just us children. Here is Bob, seven or eight, slumped in a sunsuit, squinting glumly at the camera, while I sit beside him in a dark skirt and white blouse, knees spread in abandon like the tomboy I've become, head cocked inquisitively. Bob's jaw is just slack enough to reveal a broken front tooth. He broke it and opened up one knee when, speeding down Bradford Hill, he bumped the small two-wheeler at the edge of the photo into the curb and crashed. Though no snapshot exists of the event, that's the scene forever etched in my mind: Bob limps up the driveway sobbing, as we gather around in distress. Mom coos soothing words and hands him the hanky she always keeps tucked up her sleeve, and while he wipes his streaming eyes and blows his nose, his moans subside to whimpers. Gently she bathes his knee, but when she swabs the wound with iodine, he howls like a dog until Dad, patience frazzled, begins. Don't be a crybaby, now. . . . Try to control yourself, son. . . . Try to act your age. . . . Be brave. . . . Don't snivel. . . . Growing increasingly exasperated until Mom, unable to bear another word, breaks in with quavering voice: *Stop, Sam, please, just stop now.*

These are the very words she spoke as she stood by wringing her hands while Dad, in one of his rare violent acts, tore apart my yellow cotton Easter chick shortly after we moved in. That morning, a Sunday, I had risen early and, seeing the tantalizing expanse of turquoise wall along the stairs, had taken my crayons to it while my parents slept. Part of me knew I oughtn't; part of me conveniently forgot. Waking to my handiwork, Dad—who had spent hours painting that stairwell, his ladder balanced awkwardly on the steps—seized my chick to teach me a lesson about people's property, while my suffering mother tried futilely to stop him. *Please, Sam, stop, stop!* she cried, her voice unrecognizable, like the moan of a terrified cat.

I was distraught but not devastated, as I'd been to lose my cast-iron turkey. That time I was helpless, this time I was implicated; that time I felt betrayed, this time I was the betrayer; that time I was alone, this time my mother intervened for me. Not that she could save my chick. But as I turned from one contorted face to the other, in the space between them I found myself.

Bob's thumb sucking must have started before I was born—nowadays sonograms show babies sucking in the womb. When did it stop? A teacher's note on his second-grade report card expresses concern. Unless my memory betrays him, bedtime remedies were administered in a room he didn't occupy till he was nine. First there was the bandage, big as a boxing glove, constructed each night out of mounds of gauze wound round and round his thumb and secured by adhesive tape. Next, Mom tried painting nasty-tasting stuff the color of iodine directly on his skin practically up to his wrist, while Dad held his hand steady. When that didn't work, they strapped his hand to the bedpost with bonds of gauze. These increasingly draconian measures were prescribed by our pediatrician, Dr. Silber, as each previous one failed to do the job.

What dire consequences were expected from untreated thumb sucking? When I recently asked Dad about those various cures, he sighed heavily and said, "I fear it was a cruel thing we did." If it was a matter of ruining the teeth, it didn't hold: in our family I, whose oral urges were expressed by talking rather than sucking, was the one who wore the braces, not Bob.

As I watched those ministrations from the doorway, I don't remember Bob ever protesting. I believe they were offered in a loving spirit, like any medicine—certainly by Mom, though I recall that pained expression verging on disgust in our fastidious father's eyes.

That expression on Dad's face and in his voice are what linger from those early days when I think of Bob. How unfairly memory records! Where are the daily sticks of Wrigley's Spearmint chewing gum, the pennies and nickels pulled from our ears then deposited in our palms, the magical feats of picking us up by the ears or of pulling our noses off our faces to reappear in the crotch between Dad's first two fingers? Where are the funny papers, road maps, baseball mitt, the riddles, bedtime stories, boxing and bicycle lessons, the endless games of badminton, croquet, and horseshoes Dad unstintingly bestowed on his son without complaint when he'd surely have rather been inside? They're all in there, I can pull them out at will, but they pale to insignificance beside that single pained request, accompanied by an all-suffering sigh: *Please don't whine.*

*

Was I really our father's favored child? Neither of our parents would hear of it. Yet no one could deny that Dad and I shared, in addition to genes, a private language. An antic idiom I dubbed *lawish,* it employed latinate nouns and hair-splitting logic for use in intellectual debate. Unlike today's obfuscating legalese, the despised parlance of a degraded profession representing the excesses of a litigious business society, the lawish we spoke involved exaggeration of the rhetoric of a then highly respected profession dedicated to justice. I picked it up by aping the complicated diction Dad used in reporting his cases to Mom. This so delighted him that soon we were regularly sparring in lawish for the sheer fun of it. Other children might converse in pig latin or secret code, but the language I shared with Dad was ours alone, if only because no one else recognized its charms—least of all Bob, who usually left the room in disgust when we launched into it.

Lawish was also useful for arguing my innocence or reducing my sentences, as if in a court of law. Nor was I above persuasion by poem, as in the following stanza of a long poem I composed at ten and Dad saved for half a century:

Dorothy dear, you need never fear,
Sam will take up your defense.
He'll keep everything lawful though it's ethically
* awful—*

Anything can be called "impudence."
Yet nothing restricts sentences he depicts,
For he's not only judge but he's father.
I tried to appeal, but the court is not real—
By now I should know not to bother.
Yes, a father is such a bother.

Finding such tactics irresistible, Dad quickly caved in—which confirmed Bob's bitter judgment that I could wind our father around my little finger and get away with murder. Dad adamantly denied the charge. Committed to equal justice, rather than give Bob compensatory dispensations, he urged him to develop his own verbal skills. It didn't work. Instead, Bob relied on Mom to advocate for him. On his own he substituted assertion for persuasion in a style the rest of us deemed *bossy,* or fell back on the counterproductive whine.

Had Bob known the ultimate negative effects of lawish on my writing style, which I had to work hard to undo, he might have been consoled. In my parents' attic I came upon my freshman themes from decades ago with the following criticism from my English teacher: "Although your style is fluent and mature, it tends to be stilted and pedantic." No wonder, since I learned it at Dad's elbow as he composed his briefs on long yellow pads with plenty of room for interlinear revisions at a card table he set up in the living room after dinner. As a graduate student in philosophy, I turned out papers equally convoluted. And though six years as an editor and three books for children retrained me in simplicity, to this day I relish the occasional page-long sentence I still sometimes manage to pull off.

In his speech, personal writing, and every letter he ever wrote to us, Dad's language was always elegant, subtle, precise, succinct. Yet by the end, his legal writing had grown so grotesquely mannered, so Byzantine, that his final will, cobbled together of decades' worth of codicils, had to be scrapped and redrafted by a younger lawyer in his office. As for the strenuous lawish debates that had once so intimately bound us and excluded Bob, by his tenth decade Dad's universal response to my every challenge was a weary "If you say so," even more resigned than Mom's diplomatic all-purpose rejoinder, "I'll think about it."

Chapter 4

I parked my parents' snow-covered car in a visitors' spot in the Judson garage. After signing in at the desk, I rode the elevator to the top floor, where Dad was waiting in his apartment with papers for me to sign. He was still managing their affairs and paying bills, but he wanted to give me his and Mom's powers of attorney, just in case. Though their reduced circumstances distressed me, I was excited to find that as their powers diminished mine increased.

Two white-haired women slowly bumped their walkers off the elevator. I was impressed by how long the door stayed open. After several months Judson still seemed to me satisfactory. The apartments for Independent Living were light and comfortable, overlooking either a landscaped hillside or the downtown skyline. In the spacious Fisher Dining Room friendships and love affairs flourished, producing the same gossip and backbiting as everywhere else. Even in Nursing, where personal attachments were circumscribed, aides seemed competent and kind, administrators responsive to their charges' needs. I considered my parents lucky to be able to afford it, though I knew my father suffered to see the savings of a lifetime sucked rapidly into Judson's coffers.

We had all been glad when, after a monthlong trial in

a furnished suite, Dad signed a lease on an apartment in Independent Living. Now, as he opened the door at the sound of the chime, I was again pleased by the pair of airy rooms I had furnished with their favorite things from home. How perfectly everything fit: the antique secretary, the Persian rugs, the twirling chair ridden by generations of squealing grandchildren and great-grandchildren, the marital bed, the cloisonné lamp they'd purchased on their honeymoon. The art I'd hung on the walls fit so well that even Mom, with her still exacting taste, had approved.

Dad kissed me gently on each cheek with a tenderness that seemed to grow with his frailty, and took my coat. He was dressed formally, as always, in a suit and tie, though we were only going down to visit Mom, who now occupied a room on the fifth floor of the Breuning Health Center, in the dementia ward.

They had been together in their apartment only a few weeks when suddenly, in the middle of the night, Dad, unable to breathe, had pulled the emergency cord beside their bed and was rushed to the hospital again with congestive heart failure—probably due to the increased salt in Judson's cuisine. Mom, alone and distraught, had wandered the Judson halls in her chiffon nightgown, one satin mule on her foot, one in her hand, searching for Dad and asking each person she encountered to please get her husband on the phone, his telephone number is 911. Since she could not be left alone, she was moved to a room on five which the death of the previous occupant, a Ph.D. in theology who had long served as right hand to the bishop, had just made available. As Mom's situation was considered an emergency, and she was a Judson resident, albeit by only a few weeks, she had been whisked to the top of the waiting list for the coveted room. And when Dad returned from the hospital to their apartment the following week in need of special assistance, Mom remained in Nursing.

In Dad's kitchen I found a sinkful of dirty dishes. Though for several years he'd been doing all the dishes in the Shaker house, here without a dishwasher he didn't seem to know what to do. I filled the sink with soapy water and instructed him. Afterward he sat me down to sign a pile of documents and with lawyerly authority affixed his notary seal beneath each signature.

When he excused himself to use the bathroom, I looked through the bookcase, filled with his personal selection of essential books: dictionary, thesaurus, Bartlett's *Quotations, Robert's Rules of Order,* all eleven volumes of Will and Ariel Durant's *Story of Civilization,* Cervantes, Shakespeare, Rabelais, Voltaire, and of course each of my own books, inscribed on their flyleaves. Curious, I read my inscriptions, which together presented a drastically condensed record of a quarter century of feeling. I was not surprised to see them start out cool ("For Dorothy and Sam, with love") and grow progressively warmer ("Thank you for life, devotion, everything"), until the latest one, "To my beloved parents," sizzles with "gratitude, admiration and boundless love." This is the book I dedicated to Bob. Though I felt so unconnected to him that it never occurred to me to do so while he was alive, belatedly I'd made the gesture, hoping to give some comfort to our parents.

As I flipped through my books trying to see with their eyes, I recalled how nervously I'd once anticipated their responses—especially to my first adult novel, *Memoirs of an Ex-Prom Queen,* whose heroine, born the year I was born, grows up in a suburb like my suburb in a family like my family, except that her brother is barely present and not adopted. Nothing is told about her before she enters school at five. Strictly a product of her social environment, in which the unacknowledged force of sexism operates like fate, her family is merely incidental.

But a novel is not a life, a family is not incidental.

Glancing at my other books, I recognized the hidden pattern. To conquer the need for a man is the subtext of the first, to live on one's own without anyone is what animates the last. The burden of all my work: to overcome dependency. So unquestioningly did I embrace this goal that when a lover from whose spell I was struggling to extricate myself suggested that people were not meant to be alone, I stared at him in amazement. By then I had been twice married, each time swinging between strong feelings of triumph and defeat; nevertheless, until that moment this commonplace idea had never occurred to me.

I had always connected my preoccupation with shedding my dependency to the feminist ideal of autonomy I embraced in my thirties. Now suddenly in my father's Judson apartment I recognized it as far more deeply rooted in the painful, primal challenge to leave one's parents. In the push-pull of growing up I'd gradually realized that one day, if I could find the nerve, I would leave that comfortable, narrow world of Cleveland Heights. But my very awareness of a freer life elsewhere and the confidence I needed to pursue it were my parents' gifts to me. Not that they encouraged me to leave, only to strive and attain. But if like them I were to travel a distance as great as from immigrant ghetto to the Heights, there was no place but away. To please them meant to lose them. It took me four decades and my brother's death to understand this.

"Ready?" said Dad brightly, smelling of soap. He inserted his hearing aid, took up his walker, which he'd been given upon discharge from the hospital, locked his door, and led me on the arduous route he followed daily to visit Mom. A long walk to the elevator, down one floor, another haul to a second bank of elevators, down another floor, then through heavy double doors past rows of patients lined up in their wheelchairs, their eyes glazed or their heads lolling on their chests, some cuddling teddy bears, some calling out, some dozing before the TV.

Dad was a man of such ebullient energy that even in repose he'd be either drumming his fingers or tapping his feet, burning off every calorie he consumed in steady between-meal snacking. Yet by the time we arrived at Mom's room, he was puffing. "I'm told the exercise is tonic," he assured me comfortingly.

After my first visit to Mom's room I'd wept. For a long time I'd watched her growing confusion without taking in what it meant. But in the dementia ward it finally came clear to me: that strong, capacious, worldly mind, though sunny still, was gradually shriveling, even as her dominion had shrunk from the whole of Greater Cleveland to a single small room.

Not that either of my parents complained. They always greeted me cheerfully with kisses, smiles, and reassurances. The nurses were touched by Dad's loyalty that brought him daily to visit Mom and by their open expressions of affection. Declining all group activities, they stayed to themselves in her room in adjacent chairs holding hands until sleep overcame them or it was time for him to go back up to Fisher Dining Room for lunch. Often he returned to her room in the afternoon, somehow managing to heave himself with a groan onto her high hospital bed for his accustomed afternoon nap, while she sat in her chair gazing quietly off into space until the winter light began to fade and her chin dropped to her breast and she too dozed. Sometimes they expressed their fortitude as gratitude for having come this far relatively undamaged.

Still, I wondered what they really felt about their sudden relocation to the country of old age—of frailty, weakness, heart failure, dementia, and the inescapable approach of death.

*

Accentuate the positive, obliterate the negative was our family's response to death. We had ample opportunity to practice it: someone seemed always to be dying. To me, first and worst were the deaths of mothers upon giving birth: first Bob's mother Henrietta, before I was born, then when I was five Mom's sister Jeannette, radio's Singing Lady who'd once dedicated a song to me. Growing up, I could conceive of no worse horror than the brutal manufacture of orphans: Nazis tearing infants from their mother's arms or shooting parents before their children's eyes. Slave children sold away from their parents. Families lost to each other in the smoldering rubble of the Bomb.

"Twice in one family! Imagine! How could such a thing happen?" cried my mother as we sat in her room in Breuning revisiting the past. Dementia did not diminish her outrage. "I'll never understand how that doctor could have left the hospital," she said. "Left Jeannette there to bleed to death. The rat!"

Beyond the window snow fell silently. She sighed, then switched abruptly from outrage to regret. "I should never have slept in your bed that night and allowed you to see me so upset. You were just a baby. How could you possibly understand? I should have slept somewhere else. What a terrible thing to do to you!"—blaming herself, as usual, for any pain suffered by her children.

Starting in adolescence, I found this odd side effect of maternal guilt, which rendered all my suffering my mother's fault, silly and irritating. I deplore that widespread cultural myth, described by Marilynne Robinson (whose novel *Housekeeping* depicts a childhood of shocking deprivation) as "a sort of latter-day bungled Freudianism with the idea of sublimation stripped away," according to which "one is born and in passage through childhood suffers some grave harm. Subsequent good fortune is meaningless because of this injury, while subsequent misfortune is highly significant as a consequence of this injury. The work of one's life is to discover and name the harm one has suffered." Like Robinson, I consider it "a mean little myth, far worse than most it presumes to displace." But though I always rejected Mom's claims of responsibility for whatever happened to me, even going to the other extreme of denying her her proper influence, I never denied that her grief that December night as she lay beside me sobbing for her dead sister lodged deeper in my heart than death, to reverberate forever.

Our house had been thrown into chaos, with out-of-towners from both sides of the family streaming in to stay with us. Everything was in disarray: sofa pillows were laid out on the living room floor, folding cots were carried down from the third floor, and Bob and I were told that we would have to share our beds or give them up to visitors. We took this as a chance to sleep in the trundle bed, a mysterious set of springs on wheels nestled under the studio couch, which we always vied for. After Dad flipped a coin, Bob hooted with triumph as he won the trundle bed. But I trumped him in the end by getting to sleep in our mother's arms.

It was the dark of night when I heard the sound. Something I'd never heard before. I'd been basking in the rare pleasure of feeling her soft body beside me in my narrow bed when I realized that the strange sound was coming from her. She was turned away from me, an arm thrown over her head, but I knew from her heaving shoulders that she was sobbing.

I'd never heard her cry before. Dad often cried when he read to us, but she, never. She was the strong one, our comforter.

Mommy?

She wrapped her arms around me, enfolded me in her smell.

Mommy, what's wrong?

Nothing, dearest. I'll tell you tomorrow. Go to sleep.

If she could collapse like this, then what was in store for me? Please, Mommy, I begged, as my world crumbled.

Tomorrow, love, I promise. Try to go back to sleep now.

In the morning she kept her promise. She was sad to say that Aunt Jeannette had died giving birth to my new cousin. From then on I would have two brothers.

After that night, my mother's tears always devastated me. With a single terrible exception the only times I ever saw her cry were over death or approaching death—of her siblings, her parents, her son, and when my father, diagnosed with heart failure, was given a year to live. The single exception was for me. Now, sitting between my parents in my mother's room, emboldened and humbled by the passage of time, and hoping for absolution before it was too late, I leaned forward and said, "I'm sorry for the ways I hurt you too, Mom."

"Hurt me? You? When?" She moved her swollen ankles, of which Dad (and she) had been so proud that she always wore pumps to show them off, from the hassock to the floor.

I braced myself. "Oh, for instance, when I didn't show up when you had cancer."

"Cancer? I had cancer?"

"Your sarcoma. Dr. Ross removed it."

"Is that true, Sam? Did I have cancer? Did Dr. Ross remove it?"

In the prime of her life, at fifty-two, she had discovered a small hard lump on her thigh—a result, she always believed, of a constricting panty girdle—that turned out to be a deadly sarcoma. The cancer had been a central event of her life, a great turning point, the subject of her most inspiring essay as well as the occasion of my most egregious slight. Her prognosis had been grim—at most a year to live, said the surgeon; yet I, twenty-six, newly married and living in New York, did not attend her. I had not been fully informed—or had I? True, I knew she'd had a tumor removed and would be going in for follow-up surgery, but taboo words like *cancer, sarcoma, malignant* were never spoken in our family; I had no idea she was facing death. Dad never suggested that I'd better fly to Cleveland pronto, and in the years following, no one ever reproached or even questioned me about my failure to be at my mother's side. Not until thirteen years later, when I read her article "I Was Given a Year to Live (Thirteen Years Ago)" did I realize that she had expected to die.

Finally understanding the enormity of my neglect, I'd written my parents a long, distressed letter of apology that also had elements of blame. Why hadn't they told me clearly what was going on? Why were they always so damned secretive, especially about bad news? Why hadn't they ordered me home, made me do the right thing?—this, though we all knew that my father had kept up a steady futile struggle my whole life to get me to do my duty: to write the thank-you note, remember the birthday, respond to a request, phone my brother. The more he "suggested," the more I refused—and, in my need to distinguish my desires from theirs, often made a federal case of my refusal rights.

Dissatisfied with my defensively written apology and the casual response it had sparked, on my next visit to Cleveland I'd again broached the question of my filial failure. Wanting Mom to know that it had been an inexcusable lapse of attention but not of feeling, I'd decided to offer a simple straightforward apology, without excuse or accusation, to convey the depths of my regret.

Mom and I were driving down Fairhill Road on our way to Severance Hall, where I would be using Dad's ticket to the symphony. Snow was falling in huge soggy flakes. When we stopped for a light, I turned to her and asked, How must you have felt when I wasn't there for you when you had cancer?

Instantly a single sob escaped her lips; tears filled her eyes and slid down her cheeks. Though I was in my forties then, Mom in her sixties, I felt helpless, as I had on the night Aunt Jeannette died.

I'm sorry, Mom, I said over the squeak of the windshield wipers, hoping with Kates optimism that it wasn't too late. I'm so sorry. I just didn't know.

Mom didn't speak. She neither reproached nor forgave me, just fished a hanky out of her purse and wiped her tears. Then she squared her shoulders, composed her face, produced a smile, and waited for the light to change.

"You're mistaken, dearest," Mom said now, looking at me with affection. "Even if I may once have had cancer—and Sam says I had, so I won't dispute it—you have never let me down."

I searched her face. Had she forgiven me or merely forgotten? Perhaps the pain I'd caused was too heavy for memory to bear. After so many years and so much history, maybe time itself, that famous healer of wounds, had finally run out. In the untroubled calm of Mom's soft brown eyes, now ringed with the blue of age, I saw that I would probably never know.

The out-of-towners left after the funeral and the new baby moved in with us. They named him John, after his mother Jeannette. I never questioned that he should live with us, since not only was his mother my mother's sister but his father, Uncle Abe Kates, was my father's brother. From the moment of his birth Johnny was half Davis and half Kates, like me. Dad liked to observe that genetically we were like true siblings—even closer, he implied, than Bob and I.

It seemed only fair that the nursery, with those charming children riding the stars and moons, be given over to the new baby. My crib was hauled down from the third floor for him; my grown-up twin bed was turned over to Miss Daisy, a frumpy middle-aged English nanny who, despite our family's insecure Depression income, moved into the nursery to care for Johnny while Mom went off to work; and I moved into Bob's brown plaid environment. A pair of matching cots called daybeds were installed. I haven't a single memory of Bob and me together in that room, which we shared for a good three years, except for the daybeds, which I remember vividly, down to the ink stain I made on one of the fitted green spreads. The closet, the biggest in the house, was easy to divide in half like our parents' closet; Dad built us two sets of shelves, one on each side, so we could each be responsible for keeping our possessions neat, and Bob's room became "our" room.

Suddenly we were a household of six instead of four— and sometimes seven, on those days when Bob's other sister,

Marian, came to stay with us. Or eight, if you counted the housekeeper who lived on the third floor and took care of us while our mother was downtown working at her new job with the WPA.

*

In the elegant Fisher Dining Room en route to the booth where Mom and Dad had become a fixture during their first weeks at Judson but where Dad now regularly ate alone, we were invited by three women residents to sit with them. Dad declined. "Do you ever eat with them?" I asked when we were seated.

He shook his head. "Bunch of old ladies."

"Then do you ever eat with the men?" I gestured toward the large table of a dozen men at the far end of the room.

Never having had a social life apart from Mom, Dad curled his lip and shook his head. His once red hair was now pure white, but aside from the color and the depth of the widow's peak it was still the hair of his youth, so thick and wavy that to tame it he wore a stocking cap to bed, made from Mom's cast-off hose.

After we ordered our lunch, he told me he had read my newest book, the one I'd dedicated to Bob, and was now reading it again, out loud to Mom. She'd tried it herself but had been unable to finish a single page. Always a passionate reader, at some indeterminate moment without acknowledging it she had stopped reading altogether. "Not yet, but I will," she'd say when I asked if she had looked at the magazines and library books I brought her whenever I visited. From the house I'd brought an album of family photos and books on her favorite artists, and sometimes I sat beside her on her bed slowly turning pages as she studied them, calling out in recognition the names of her beloved siblings and artists—as if they were her alphabet and she a child excitedly learning to read. But she never picked them up on her own. "Maybe later," she would say when I suggested it. Even her mail remained unopened beside her bed until one of us read it to her. There was nothing to be done but accept this change like all the others she'd undergone and appreciate what powers remained.

When Dad and I returned to Mom's room after lunch, we found her sitting on her bed listening attentively to an attractive silver-maned man with a leonine head seated in a wheelchair, volubly holding forth. Seeing us at the door, Mom, ever the gracious hostess, made the introductions. "I'm Dorothy Kates. This is my daughter Alix," she said, waving toward me, "and this—"

Before she introduced Dad, he moved to her side, laid a proprietary hand on her arm, and forcefully interjected, "I'm her husband, *Mister* Kates."

The visitor, undeterred, continued his animated talk. I tried to follow what he said, but after a few minutes I realized that his words made no sense. The language was English, with its familiar grammar, vocabulary, and inflections, but the sentences lacked all discernible meaning. Still, Mom listened with seemingly rapt attention, nodding periodically and using all her social skills to make the stranger feel at home.

She seemed so self-possessed that I wondered if she really belonged here. To me she was nothing like the other dementia patients who sat in their wheelchairs staring blankly into space, or unzipped their flies to flash their organs, or clutched at me as I walked by. When we sat talking in her room, she was herself: interested in everything we said, full of detailed reminiscences, with all her grace and beauty intact. There was only a trace of grey in her fine dark hair, her bright eyes were responsive, and her skin was surprisingly smooth and taut over her dramatic Tartar bones. Like her own mother, who in her nineties had passed for seventy at the Golden Age Lounge, Mom looked strikingly younger than anyone else on five, though in fact she was older than many by a decade or more.

Dad had begun to tap his foot impatiently when a nurse burst into the room. "Oh, there you are, Mr. Feingold! We've been looking all over for you. Time for your medicine." As she wheeled his chair around toward the door, he waved and smiled at Mom, uttering sounds I took to mean he would return.

I wasn't surprised. Even on the fifth floor of Judson, where memory was at a minimum and the ratio of men to women was one to ten, it was my mother whom Mr. Feingold had singled out to court.

*

Death had claimed two mothers in our family before I was six, giving me two brothers and leaving me hyperaware of the great but fragile privilege of possessing both my natural parents. In that orphan-ridden family I dreaded being next. So tuned was I to death that Dad had to change the last verse of "Rock-a-bye Baby" for me because the original frightened me with its intimations of death: instead of, "when the bough breaks the cradle will fall and down will come baby cradle and all" our family sang, "when the bough bends we'll all take a peek to see if our baby is fast asleep." Similarly, in place of "Now I Lay Me Down to Sleep," the prayer I brought home from kindergarten, which upset me with the line "if I should die before I wake" (and upset Dad, an atheist, with its *Lords* and *souls*), Dad, who would not hesitate to rewrite the world if necessary to protect us, concocted our own prayer:

> *Now I lay my head on my pillow so white*
> *And hope I sleep well throughout the night.*
> *And when I wake tomorrow morn*
> *I hope I'll be happy and not forlorn.*

When Bob cried, which he did whenever he hurt himself, he received a salutary lecture from Dad on self-control—one of the liabilities, I observed, of being a boy. When I cried, usually in secret and deliberately, I received no lectures. I wept from sentiment rather than pain—like Dad himself, who though otherwise dry-eyed would frequently have to pull his big white hanky out of his pocket, shake it open, and reach under his glasses to wipe his eyes during the dramatic readings of poems and stories by Longfellow, Stevenson, Whitman, and Poe with which he nightly put us to bed. He claimed it was something in the timbre of his voice that opened his tear ducts, but I wonder if it wasn't the feelings. In face of certain emotions I too was able to hold my throat muscles in such a way and throw my voice into such a register as to create a lump in my throat that could trigger sweet cathartic tears. Not for show but for my own private delectation. Even lyrics about lesser losses than death could start my tears flowing:

> *Oh my darling Nellie Grey*
> *They have taken you away*
> *And I'll never see my darling anymore.*
> *They have taken you to Georgia*
> *Where you'll work your life away*
> *And I'll never see my darling anymore.*

I had only to sing this over to myself, with its wrenching final line, to bring the desired effect. I didn't understand that it was about slavery; I only knew it was about loss. There was no mystery as to what made me cry in my private tearjerker, the popular "I'm Nobody's Baby," now that Johnny had replaced me as the baby in the family:

I'm nobody's baby,
I wonder why.
Each night and day I pray the lord up above
Please send me down somebody to love.
But nobody wants me,
I'm blue somehow,
Won't someone hear my plea
And take a chance with me,
Because I'm nobody's baby now.

It was my father, not my mother, whom I imagined losing when I cried myself to sleep. Losing a mother was too close to home to try out even in fantasy. A recurring dream that my father died was so real to me that for days following it I had to pad down to my parents' room in the middle of the night to reassure myself that it was, as they unwaveringly insisted, only a dream.

Johnny was a fat baby with pale silky straw-colored ringlets, merry blue eyes (which like mine would turn hazel-green at puberty), a dribbling lower lip, and rolls of tender, pinchable fat at his neck, his wrists, his thighs and feet. Every night at dinner he banged his high chair with his spoon, shouting, Mo meat! Mo meat!

On weekends, Uncle Abe, his father, who had a drugstore with a soda fountain, took Johnny out in his black

Plymouth coupé for ice cream and teased us children with riddles and rhymes of which Dad disapproved: *Inch Me and Pinch Me sat on a fence. Inch Me fell off. Who was left?* Or:

> *A peanut sat on a railroad track*
> *His heart was all aflutter.*
> *A railroad train came whizzing by—*
> *Toot! toot! Peanut butter.*

Between Uncle Abe's visits I pretended Johnny was mine. After school I liked to push him around the kitchen in his walker, bounce him in his bouncer, feed him raisins, teach him "One Potato, Two Potato," and blow raspberries into his pudgy neck to make him laugh. A fat jolly boy, he made us seem like a big ordinary family. Our Kates family Christmas card from 1939 pictures five cartoon figures racing in a line toward the open edge of the card, each identified beneath by name: Sam is running at the front of the line; Dorothy, arms pumping, runs after him; Bob is pedaling his bicycle; I'm zipping along on a scooter; and little Johnny with a halo of curls brings up the tail on his kiddy car. It was as one big family that we attended reunion picnics, family seders, and the ceremony at which Mom and her sister Celia finally received their bachelor's degrees. Miss Daisy stood Johnny on her lap so he could see them as they marched slowly down the aisle of Severance Hall in black gowns and what looked like tasseled notebooks on their heads, to the strains of a stately march. When they came alongside us en route to the distant stage, Mom blew us kisses and Aunt Celia sent us little finger waves.

Then one day Uncle Abe remarried and took Johnny back. He came in his black Plymouth coupé with his new wife, Rhea (a first cousin of Mom and Jeannette; might as well keep it in the family). After he parked, Rhea got out and held out her arms as Mom carried Johnny toward them. Johnny started to bawl and clung to Mom. He wouldn't even go to Uncle Abe. Mom held him while Uncle Abe loaded Johnny's suitcase and equipment in the back. Then they tried again, but Johnny still refused to go. Finally Uncle Abe just took him.

In my mind I see him still, that jolly three-year-old, stretching out his dimpled arms and wailing for Mom. Flanked on either side by Bob and me, Mom stood on the sidewalk waving goodbye to Johnny and smiling encouragingly. Uncle Abe put him in Rhea's lap and shut the door, then went around to the driver's side and started up the car. Johnny had lost one mother to death; now before my eyes he lost another to marriage, and there was nothing to be done about it.

On the sidewalk Mom kept waving and smiling despite the tremble of her lip until the black coupé disappeared over Bradford Hill. Then she took Bob and me by the hand, and we three walked slowly back into the house. Before long, my baby brother became just another cousin, thin and sad. *And I'll never see my darling anymore.*

Chapter 5

A New Yorker, a dweller in large apartment buildings, I never owned a house. When anything needs fixing, I call the super. Once, in the 1960s, my husband and I almost went in with some friends to buy and renovate a dilapidated brownstone on a tree-lined block in Chelsea, but I nixed it. What would we do when the roof leaked or the foundations crumbled? Suppose the wiring or plumbing went haywire? What if rats moved into the basement or the stairs sagged? I didn't want the responsibility.

Now my time had come. The Shaker house had to be sold. With Bob gone, the job fell to me.

Before I could put the house on the market, it had to pass muster with the building inspector—Shaker Heights's way of "preserving the tax base." A preliminary inspection produced a list of violations from roof to cellar five pages long. To correct them would require the services of a roofer, carpenter, plumber, electrician, glazier, screener, tiler, painter, paper hanger, plasterer, exterminator, stonemason, ironworker, locksmith, garage-door repairer, gardener, asphalt pourer, and tuck pointer. I was flabbergasted: out of pride Mom had kept the house looking spiffy, and out of prudence Dad had kept it in good repair. But the inspector's ruling was nonnegotiable.

I launched a series of brief packed visits to Cleveland to meet with workers and contractors, get estimates and bids, and in between try to squeeze order from the chaos of forty years of life and accumulation. To determine the value of what was there, I consulted curators, antique dealers, liquidators, and arcane specialists who all vied with one another for a cut of this lucrative stash. And there were the finances to oversee, advisors to consult, tax and insurance records to compile, transfer papers to submit, wills to have redrawn.

My New York friends commiserated with me over each alarming development in the steadily expanding occupation that took me ever more frequently to Cleveland. Though a few had already lost parents, most were oblivious of what was coming. Like expectant mothers who no matter how thoroughly they think they have prepared haven't a clue to what's in store, they wavered between innocence and dismay. After a group of feminist friends began holding meetings about establishing a feminist retirement home in Manhattan, words like *dementia, Alzheimer's,* and *nursing home* were quickly quashed as irrelevant to our project. (Until last year those scary words had spooked me too.) Our home was to be for people with all their faculties, who as they aged might wish to spend their later years in a community of the like-minded. I agreed with the group consensus that we view aging as ripening rather than decline and was excited to learn that all over town other groups of midlife feminists like us, who as young women had agitated for legalized abortion, equal pay for equal work, and universal childcare, were once more taking charge of our futures. But in light of my new knowledge I thought my friends were ignoring something crucial by seeing my task as a burdensome distraction from my life.

They were wrong. The truth was, I was now utterly absorbed; nothing I'd ever done was more absorbing. One friend urged me to hire a general contractor to oversee the repairs, but I declined. I wanted to do everything myself. That I was a writer and this crisis now my subject was only part of the reward; more gratifying still was my knowledge that after so many years of disregard I was finally coming through for my parents. Every day I sensed the irony that this fulfillment would have escaped me if Bob had lived. Engrossed in my distant New York life, with Bob around to do the work, I would have failed to respond to our parents' crises until the last minute. Then I would have missed the delectable pleasure of hearing my name instead of Bob's on our father's lips as, gently cupping my chin in a palm as redolent as ever of soap and witch hazel, and grinning gold, he announced to everyone, "I don't know how we'd ever manage without Alix."

Once my daytime labors were over, I could barely wait to resume my nighttime investigations of the house. The drawers were full of snapshots, clippings, letters, manuscripts, records. Delving into them, I was sometimes so overcome by emotion that I had to stop—that's what your family can do to you.

Not that mine is especially sad. Despite the early deaths and sorrows, the occasional scandal and suicide, there were far more winners than losers; most were long lived, strong willed, productive, encompassing in two generations—from the last decade of the nineteenth century, when my penniless grandparents emigrated from Eastern Europe, to the last decade of the twentieth, when the last of their children were dying—a vast range of human experience. As I filled page after page with notes, fired by curiosity and excitement, I felt that when my work was done, the house sold, and the estates in order, I would have earned the equivalent of a Ph.D. in some unacknowledged discipline—life studies? estate management? filial devotion? some interdisciplinary combination? In my zeal I barely stopped to eat, and more than once I surfaced from deep immersion in the files to see dawn break like a wave over the snowy garden without my having been to bed.

Still, if it had not been mine, would I have been so absorbed by this family? Impossible *if*!—exact opposite of the cold-blooded doctrine with which as a youth I'd condemned family and blood allegiance as special pleading. Perhaps my odd creed had been an attempt to make myself equal with Bob, knowing that only an equal could compete and win: if such bonds carried no special weight then my connection to our parents was no firmer than his.

Whatever my motive, that irrational denial of family ties was undermined by my ineluctable feelings of attachment. Their force amazed me when I came upon an agonizing letter I had written to my mother two years after her cancer, while I was pregnant with my first child. Rereading it after so many years, I felt the ancient pain of separation flood back through my veins and—I couldn't help it—I cried again. I cried for her and for myself and for my own children whose turn would be upon them before they knew it.

> You say you hurt and I hurt you; you say you always loved me too much. It breaks my heart. I know it must be true, and when I allow it to penetrate it breaks me up. I know it must be true because I always loved you too much. One of the common reactions to recognizing that you love too much, to recognizing that you are extremely vulnerable, is to pull away, throw up a

protective wall. It's what I've tried to do over the years, sort of out of desperation. The wall, however, is very flimsy; it creates the illusion of protection only when no one approaches it, but when someone nears I know it's as good as nonexistent, and I panic. You should see that the colder I am to you, the more evident that my loving you is too much, more than I can handle.

I've had a good life and suffered relatively little hurt. Because of this, to me remorse is the cruellest pain: I haven't known much other pain. I learned it somehow out of my relationship with you and Dad: you were always so good to me and so loving and so lovable and so forgiving, while I was not so very good; I wasn't worthy of such affection and understanding. Now, I know that I wasn't very bad either, but judgment hasn't much to do with it. I seem always to have been waiting for the axe to fall, but it has never fallen. What I do that hurts you is, in my clumsy way, to stave off the axe. It was at first a temporary expedient, like my staying out of town; now it's a relatively comfortable modus vivendi, the original purpose of which sI have tried fairly successfully to lose sight of. Of course, the result of losing sight of it is that when the axe threatens (and your showing me affection is the threat) I try in the only way that's immediately available to stave it off: I run. (This is a clumsy metaphor, but the feelings it is to convey are diffuse and difficult to pinpoint.) . . .

In sum, I love you. It's harder and harder to show, but as true as ever. I'm sorry I hurt you, but I don't know how to avoid it. I can't talk of turning over new leaves because I don't know what's on the next page.

Besides, I know you're not concerned with pleas-
antries and appearances, but rather with the feelings
inside. Just reflect how obviously I loved you when we
lived together and how loving you've always been and
you'll know it can't have changed. I'm sure you must
know it; I count on your knowing it. There never was
closer mother and daughter. . . .

Explaining but doing nothing; afraid to lose myself to
love; too shaky in my identity to change; not even saving
Mom's reply. Now, seeing my letters so carefully preserved,
I regretted having saved so few of hers, and worse, having
often cringed to read them. Sometimes, I remembered,
when those pale blue envelopes arrived in the mail, addressed in that hand so like my own, I would put them
aside for days before I could open them, then skim them
quickly and throw them out, embarrassed or overwhelmed
by their emotion.

Now suddenly I was avid to preserve her papers, as I'd
rescued my father's when he'd vacated his office—as if saving their works for posterity could redeem my neglect.
Otherwise, their lives would simply vanish—like the family's mother tongue, Yiddish, brought to Cleveland from
Poland, Lithuania, and Russia by my grandparents only to
die in the birth pangs of my generation. Gone. And next—
the family's memories and secrets unless I somehow rescued them.

How lucky, then, I thought, to be a writer attempting to
stall the disappearance of the ephemeral, squeeze meaning
from the detritus of memory, preserve a bit of the fading
past. That I must violate my family's privacy and betray
their secrets seemed a small price to pay for rescuing them
from oblivion. After all, I told myself, my book would not

be published till all the principals and their enemies were dead. I intended the work as an act of preservation, but I didn't delude myself into believing that my family, should they read it, would approve. Fortunately their approval was not required.

∗

"Who's that, Daddy?" I asked, pointing to a strange face.

"Let me see now," he said, drawing back his chin and adjusting his trifocals to study a packet of photos of a Davis picnic in a Pennsylvania cornfield.

Before leaving the house I'd stuffed a large folder with snapshots to show my parents in hopes of identifying the faces before they reverted to mere generic types or representatives of an era, like the turn-of-the-century photos I'd bought in a secondhand store to decorate my seaside cabin. These snapshots were from the late 1930s and early 1940s—I could tell by the running boards and rumble seats on my uncles' cars and by the flared jackets and sweetheart necklines I had spent so many hours copying from catalogues, trying to learn how to draw people, never suspecting the styles would disappear before I had mastered the curve of a hip. Pictures of us as children, of our parents in their youth, of their siblings, and their parents too—all taking time out from their fiercely lived lives to pose before the camera.

"I'm not sure. Could be Clarence Geller, who courted your mother."

"Who?" said Mom, leaning over. "What Clarence? Let me see."

Systematically I quizzed them on every picture, recording all the names on the backs, including those of people I recognized only by a strong chin shared with Bob or an arched eyebrow with me. Though I considered this a rescue operation, I was unsettled by the paradox of memory that had troubled me since I began to write. I think of my memory as a secret storeroom at the heart of a maze; there's only one key, and I have it. Behind the door my memories rest like dormant seeds full of potential second life that can't begin till I shine light on them. Like the record of the past preserved in lava and ice, in wrecks and ruins, my memories are safe there—for the time being. But like buried treasure that turns to dust when it hits the air, once memories are delivered from private custody to the world, they become endangered. Touch them back to life, and like everything alive they begin the inescapable process of corruption, confusion, decay, the end of which is rigor mortis. As Italo Calvino succinctly put it, memory "is true only as long as you do not set it, as long as it is not enclosed in a form." While they remain private and unanalyzed, memories have all the magic and power of imagination itself. But once you seize and pin them down, once you snap the picture or write the book, they lose their shimmering complexity, their rich associations, their resonance and ambiguity until, diminished and degraded, they are lost as surely as if synapses had been destroyed, and you can no longer distinguish what's true from what's been depicted. The work, having fattened on memory, may acquire a life of its own, but the memories lie on the ground inert, like desiccated husks. This is why after I've plundered my memories for a story I can no longer tell what really took place—as prisoners forced to spill their secrets are said to lose their power to know the truth.

"Yes," said Dad, "I'm sure that's Clarence Geller. I wonder who invited him to our picnic."

At ninety-three Dad still recognized everyone, down to

the second and third cousins. His life was continuous—unlike mine, which had a gap at its center, opened when I left Cleveland, that I was only now attempting to fill.

I flipped a page to see Grandma and Grandpa Davis, now many years dead, sitting on folding camp chairs grinning into the camera. Off to the side Bob holds a baseball bat. He can't be more than eight or nine because Johnny there, peeking out from behind our mother's legs, looks about two or three. We have driven in a caravan across Ohio and into Pennsylvania to meet the Pittsburgh contingent of our clan. An hour before we arrived at this farm, the Pittsburghers had selected it as the ideal cornfield for our picnic. After striking a deal with the farmer (who could hardly refuse, since for all anyone knew the Depression could continue for another decade), they'd returned to a prearranged rendezvous to lead us here. The borrowed cauldron has been filled with water and the fire built, and while Uncle Abe tends it, the rest of us fan out through the fields to harvest the corn. Each of the hundred ears we need for this feast must be picked, shucked, and rushed to the pot in order to meet our standard of no more than fifteen minutes between field and fire. After that, explains Uncle Leon (who has begun giving me violin lessons on Saturdays), the sugar turns to starch, that's why—and since there is no snapshot of this instant to contradict me, I remember his gently tweaking my ear. The rest of the food we've brought with us: potato salad, huge seeded sour rye breads, Grandma's buttery pastries from Cleveland, cold cuts from the Pennsylvania side, and bagfuls of fresh fruit—peaches, plums, and blood-dark cherries—purchased at roadside stands along the way. But for all this fare, it's the corn that counts. And soon we'll find out who can eat the most. Some are typewriter eaters who eat across the rows, some are

toilet-paper rollers who keep turning the cob. A typewriter,
like Mom, I lost a tooth one year while gnawing corn, but
now my second teeth are firmly in—big and strong and ser-
rated. Though Grandma Davis (who came to this country
at nineteen, rolled cigars for the train fare to Cleveland, and
lived to be one hundred) almost always wins, packing away
the first dozen ears in record time with everyone cheering
her along, and Bob is catching up with her, this year I'm
ready to take them on.

My memories of those picnics are bittersweet because the
road to and from Pennsylvania led straight past Belfaire,
the Jewish orphanage. Whenever we approached it, I felt a
guilty dread. A sprawling collection of red brick buildings
on Fairmont Boulevard, Belfaire was divided into "cot-
tages" in each of which lived ten orphans segregated by age
and sex, together with a "cottage mother" and "father,"
whom we presumed were to real parents what substitutes
were to teachers. Duck! we shouted, crouching down in the
back of the car and holding our breath to avoid contamina-
tion, as we did near cemeteries. To spare my brother's feelings I would have preferred to look away and ignore the
place instead of calling attention to it. But once we had
taken over that common practice from other children, our
normalcy demanded that we duck too.

For a while some of the Belfaire children were bused to
Canterbury School in a wood-paneled station wagon,
which usually arrived just after the final bell. When Mickey
Oppenheimer, our class orphan, came tiptoeing into our
room after everyone else was seated, Miss Hamilton gave
him an indulgent nod instead of the icy reprimand ac-
corded other latecomers.

I observed Mickey closely. He never raised his hand,

passed no notes or spitballs, had no friends for partners in the daily lineups, and ate his bag lunch with the teachers and his Belfaire "brothers" and "sisters," though it was said that somewhere he had a *real* sister who lived outside the orphanage. In our family, were we like Belfaire siblings or real ones? To our parents we were unquestionably real ones, but what did Bob think? Who was his real sister, me or Marian? He'd begun to bully me, like a real brother, but treated Marian politely—did that tell? And Johnny—had he switched his feelings from Mom to Rhea? In the two years Mickey Oppenheimer was in my class after I skipped from second grade over 3B straight to 3A, I studied him for clues. But despite my lurid fascination, I learned nothing.

Today a superhighway goes to Pennsylvania, bypassing Belfaire, now surrounded by houses. Still, the buildings look pretty much as I remember them. The sign at the entrance no longer calls Belfaire an orphanage but rather a Juvenile Residential Treatment Center—just as the building across the street from my New York loft is no longer named St. Zita's Home for Friendless Women, though over the door I can still make out the painted-over letters of the discredited name, and it continues to house single expectant mothers.

*

Once Johnny left us and Miss Daisy was let go, I expected to reclaim the nursery. Everyone agreed that the room I'd shared with Bob was more desirable, situated on a corner with airy gable windows on two walls and that deep walk-in closet. But though I was eight—and mature enough to have skipped a grade—I hankered to sleep again among my children of the sky.

It was just then that Bob, who still sucked his thumb,

mumbled, whined, and bit his nails, succumbed to yet another malady. After months of tests involving nasty needles stuck in both his arms, he was pronounced Allergic. Not only to beef, lamb, and (unlucky boy!) chocolate, but to dust. Dust! that sat on every chair and table, and danced in the air we breathed—I clearly saw it whenever the sun streamed through a crack in the living room drapes. How could he avoid inhaling it with every breath? Indeed, the needle doctor hinted my brother might turn out to be allergic to himself! It was decreed that his mattress and pillow be made of foam rubber and covered with rubber sheets, that he have no rug or upholstery, none but straight wooden chairs, no curtains at his window, and, through vigilant daily vacuuming, no mote of dust in his room. The corner room we'd shared, with its several windows and wall-to-wall carpeting, was impossible to keep dust-free, so when the crib had been returned to the third floor, and the wallpaper children mercilessly buried beneath a double coat of blind white paint, Bob moved into the more manageable nursery with its single window and bare floor, and I kept the corner room.

I took over Bob's rightful room, but he was still, would always be, the elder. My big gruff noisy brother. He had a pocketknife I was not allowed to play with, though sometimes in secret, as he practiced his mumblety-peg, he permitted me to try, knowing I'd fail to make it stick in the ground. His marbles were better than mine, of which he quickly stripped me whenever he deigned to play. He mastered all the knots in the *Boy Scout Handbook;* I mastered none. He could rock-the-cradle, go over-the-falls and around-the-world with his yo-yo, while I could barely walk-the-dog. He could blow larger bubbles than I and make Life Savers last in his mouth until, paper thin, they melted away to nothing, while I impetuously chewed mine up. When we played croquet, he chose to send my ball flying to kingdom come rather than take an extra turn. He kept his map collection locked in his bottom drawer and knew the capital of every state. He could hit a baseball, make a touchdown, run faster, yell louder, whistle longer, laugh harder, spit farther, fight meaner than I, and he could write his name in the snow in urine. Some things I did better than he: draw, dance, act, make music, scheme, and, most important, read. Still, he was always ahead of me in school, and long before I, he was permitted to cross the street, stay out late, ride the streetcar by himself, drive our parents' car.

I wonder what he thought when I skipped 3B, narrowing his advantage over me from a year to a single semester. He never told me. He told me very little, ever, though I was known as a pest for my persistent questions. What did he think about his mother Henrietta? What did he think about his father Papadear? What did he think about his sister Marian, living with our elderly grandparents? What did he think about Johnny, whose mother, like his own, had died in childbirth? Johnny once confided that he'd always felt guilty for causing his mother's death, but Bob never said a word. What did he think about the orphans in our school bused in from Belfaire? What did he think about his room? his bed with rubber sheets? his allergies to beef, lamb, chocolate, and dust? What did he think about his Boy Scout knots, his baseball bat and catcher's mitt, his football helmet and shoulder pads, his reindeer sweater, his bicycle, his roadmaps locked in a bottom drawer, his paper route, his broken tooth? What did he think about his childhood? About Mom and Dad? About me?

I don't know the answers to these questions. Though we played footsies under the table at hundreds of meals, and walked together up Bradford Hill to school scores of times, and spent long summer afternoons on the back porch eating fruit and Oreos, playing Karems and War, and wrestled hard in the living room, once we started school he never said much of anything to me except, Give in? and Wanna bet? and I'm gonna tell! and None of your beeswax.

*

At Sunday dinner in Fisher Dining Room, Dad and I skipped dessert in favor of birthday cake with Mom. The following month she would turn eighty-eight. Since I was leaving for New York that night and uncertain when I'd next be back, we decided to celebrate today. It hardly mattered, as Mom had lost her sense of time.

In her room I poured dining hall decaf and lit candles on a chocolate cake I'd bought at a bakery that afternoon. Whenever I came to visit now, I brought my parents chocolate, which they usually devoured on the spot. In the past year Mom's appetite had so diminished that she was nearly as thin as Dad; yet the two of them could consume a pound of Oreos in a single sitting.

After we finished singing "Happy Birthday," Mom asked me, "What birthday is this?"

"Guess."

"Eighty-five?"

"Pretty close. Eighty-eight."

"Eighty-eight!" she said, amazed. "Can it be?"

"Do you find that hard, Mom?"

"Do I find what hard, dear?"

"Everything. Turning eighty-eight. Being here at Judson."

Mom gazed far off beyond the snow-filled window and didn't answer. It was only months since she'd agreed to trade her large Shaker house, where she had reigned for forty years, for the small apartment in Judson Park. We had convinced her to move by telling her that Dad's health required it. This was true, in the sense that caring for her at home, cooking her meals, getting her to take her medicines, helping her to the bathroom, arranging for snow to be shoveled and groceries to be delivered—in short, doing all the tasks she could no longer do and he was unable to delegate to the aides I'd hired to care for them—had become too much of a strain on his failing heart. For his part, he believed the move to Judson was for Mom's sake, which was also true and daily growing truer as she lost more and more brain cells, needed more and more care.

When Mom didn't answer, I tried another tack. Choice was beyond her, so I broke my question down. "How does it feel to be here at Judson?"

Mom turned to Dad, whom she had appointed her voice when her memory and judgment began to go. "How do we feel, Bummer?"

I gave my father a warning look. I'd been trying to get him to let her speak for herself, though it made him feel he was letting her down. "I can't answer for you," he said sheepishly. "How do you feel, Bummer?"

"How do I feel?" she repeated. She filled a pause with ardent thought and said, snapping her head in a familiar, decisive gesture, "I accept it."

Both my parents were accomplished accepters. Adaptation and acceptance were my priceless heritage.

"And how does it feel to be eighty-eight?" I asked.

"I like it," she said. "It certainly beats the alternative." She'd been giving a similar answer since her seventies, but this time, leaning forward, she added a new caveat: "Though if the truth be known, I'd rather be eighty-two."

Of course she'd select eighty-two! She had still been game at eighty-two, singing at my wedding in an elegant grey silk suit. She had still been tough at eighty-two, searching out cancer cures for Bob. Then a week after the wedding he died, and everything changed. "What a cruel hoax of fate that he is dead and I live," she wrote to me bitterly. Gradually she stopped bothering to answer her mail, then to comb her hair, brush her teeth, cream her face, take her pills. Finally she stopped showering or getting dressed.

Dad took a bite of cake and a swig of decaf and wiped his mouth on a paper napkin. "Don't forget, Bummer, your mother lived to a hundred. Mine lived only to eighty-seven."

Then, flashing what Dad had been calling her ten-thousand-dollar smile ever since she'd had all her teeth capped a few years earlier, Mom said, chuckling, "Imagine! Here we are trading longevity stories."

"You sound pretty happy," I observed.

"I am," said Mom. "I've never been depressive. None of us has. We're pretty lucky that way."

At that moment, enjoying our intimate party, I couldn't disagree. Yet it crossed my mind that if Bob had been there too we might not have felt so lucky. Like Uncle Abe, whom Dad described in his memoir as "the hard luck member of my family" ("When Abe was in high school," wrote Dad, "a truck ran over one of his feet, creating a permanent limp. When he was about 23, an automobile ran over the curb and pinned him against a building while he was waiting for a street car, costing Abe the sight of one eye. Abe's wife Jeannette died in childbirth and his second wife, Rhea, became very ill not long after she and Abe were married, and had a leg amputated. After her death Abe was placed in a nursing home where he died at age 82, blind, deaf, and mentally incompetent."), Bob was the unlucky one in ours. His first mother had died on him, he was sickly and allergic, and he had the bad luck to be an indifferent reader in a family of readers. The year we all took up reading aloud together after dinner, passing the book from hand to hand, Bob dropped out on the third session, even though it was to satisfy his teachers that our parents proposed the reading sessions in the first place. Like Dad's other stratagems to bring Bob up to standard when exhortation failed, it didn't work—no more than the desperate scheme to improve Bob's study habits by offering us cash for grades. At ten dollars a nail Bob had eventually managed to grow out his fingernails, but when it came to grades the plan backfired since I invariably collected more than he, which only confirmed his failure no matter how hard he may have tried.

Right up to the end he was unlucky, dying prematurely of lung cancer, even though he had mainly smoked a pipe—whereas I had smoked two packs of unfiltered cigarettes a day for two decades until I gave them up cold turkey in the late 1960s, and Mom, who'd smoked right up through the 1970s, had been the biggest smoker of us all. Like all the glamorous Davis women, she had smoked incessantly—Lucky Strikes, Chesterfields, Camels—anything but dowdy Kools. In most every picture from the 1940s, there they are, those dark-haired Davises, with their penciled eyebrows, their Garbo cheekbones and high-bridged noses, their heads at dashing angles, with cigarettes glowing between their long, manicured fingers. During the war, when cigarettes were rationed, resourceful Mom supplemented her meager supply by hand-rolling her own on a little leather machine after Uncle Abe, who owned a drugstore, refused to sell her cigarettes by the carton as she'd bought them before the war, but only by the pack. She was livid: There was nothing illegal about selling her more. And after all she'd done for *him*! But his stock was short, he explained, his supply uncertain, and justice demanded that he distribute what stock he had evenly among all his customers. Even after she gave up cigarettes for good, she continued to besport herself like a smoker, throwing back her head to exhale, moving her manicured fingers through the air in an elegant arc to make a point. The Kateses, on the other hand, were respectable ambitious straight-laced men and women for whom tobacco held little appeal. Dad once tried a pipe but found the whole ritual, with all its ancillary paraphernalia, too much trouble. Dad's older brother, Dr. Louis Katz, was one of the first scientists to establish the link between heart disease and smoking (and, later, cholesterol). From his elevation as head of the celebrated heart lab at Michael Reese Hospital in Chicago, where his research staff occupied an entire floor, and later as president of the American Heart Association, he shook his finger at the world, urging everyone to stop smoking. For years we all ignored him, but Bob was the one who died.

Back in Dad's apartment, I got up the nerve to ask him, "How did you and Mom feel when I stayed away all those years?"

He gave me such a searching look that I thought he might finally level with me. I was ready to take it. But he simply shrugged his shoulders and said matter-of-factly, "Naturally we didn't like it much."

It might have been prudence that made him spare me the brunt of their resentment, or maybe simple kindness. But it's also possible that their lives were less bruised by my absence than I'd grown to believe.

Emboldened by my own relentless questioning, Dad adjusted his hearing aid, nervously cleared his throat, and asked, "And your childhood—would you say it was a happy one?"

I might have given him the long answer. I might have launched a real conversation. But seeing the apprehension in his eyes as he hung on my words, all I could reply was *yes.*

Dad in his first law office, c. 1925

Bob stealing a kiss from me, 1935

The portraits of me and Bob,
in our mid-forties, that sat on Dad's dresser

Mom, on the one hundredth anniversary of the first
Women's Rights Convention in Seneca Falls, N.Y.,
in 1848, modeling a copy of a dress worn by
Elizabeth Cady Stanton

Mom and Dad on the Davis lawn following their second wedding, July 16, 1929

Expressing myself at a Davis picnic, c. 1940

Mom, Celia, and Rosemary, three of the five Davis sisters, 1945

Papadear, Bob's other father, c. 1924

Mom, c. 1930

The Kates family, c. 1926. Standing from left: Eva, Dad, Mame, Dr. Louis Katz, Sophie, Johnny's father Abe. My grandparents are seated.

*Bob's wedding, August 3, 1958. I'm at the far left,
and our parents are at the right.*

*Mom, 81, and Dad, 87, in their Shaker living room, with
works by Robert Motherwell and Franz Kline, 1988*

Chapter 6

Odd to find myself growing attached to a house I'd never lived in, where the longest I'd ever stayed was a long weekend. My children had sometimes spent a week or two with their grandparents while their father and I went traveling, but I tried to fly in and out as quickly as I could. To me home had always been the small house on Ashurst Road from which, in the late summer of 1937, only months before Johnny was born, my brother and I enrolled in Canterbury Elementary School, freeing our mother to place an ad in the "Help Wanted, Female" column of the *Cleveland Plain Dealer* for a live-in woman with excellent references to do housework and childcare in exchange for private room and bath, board, a modest wage, and Saturday afternoons and Sundays off. With her children at last in school, Mom was free to accept the tantalizing job offer that promised to lift her out of suburban sloth into the stimulating world of work.

Before her marriage she'd always worked: as a salesclerk at the May Company all through high school; then, after two years of normal school (a term of provocative metaphorical significance), teaching third and fourth grades in the Cleveland system. But in the late 1920s, local laws prohibited married women from teaching in the public schools—presumably because marriage implies sex, which when pregnancy occurs might provoke embarrassing questions in the young. Unable to choose between job and marriage, Mom elected both by eloping with my father to a secret marriage at twenty-two, four months before a second, public ceremony.

Why two weddings? I sometimes asked—as if the answer weren't obvious. Mom: I didn't want to be fired. Dad: We didn't want to wait. Sex: the untamable force that had kept my grandmothers producing children until one had borne seven, the other eight (of whom six survived). Sex was certainly on the mind of the New York justice of the peace who handed Mom the signed marriage certificate with the warning, Hang on to this young lady, you're probably going to need it, while for Dad he had only a suspicious scowl.

Decades later, after I'd published the locally scandalous *Memoirs of an Ex-Prom Queen,* and sex was finally on the table between us, my mother confessed to me that their sex life had been troubled from the start. Leaning close to confide her secret, she said, Of course, you must never repeat this, but . . .

What went wrong? Certainly not Dad's desire. Eavesdropping through the years, I heard tell that he tried to kiss Mom's sister Celia while Mom was giving birth to me; that he was once caught kissing the maid, which cost her her job; and that he was several times discovered chasing a secretary around a desk. Yet even his kisses failed. He told me that the night he met Mom, on a double date, his own date was disgusted by his awkward kisses. "The first time I kissed a girl was at a high school basketball game," he wrote in the brief memoir he composed at eighty-eight. "A splendid shot had been made by one of our players, and while everyone was cheering I sneaked a kiss to the cheek of a very pretty twin, who was not even aware I had done so"—as if a kiss that doesn't register can count as a kiss.

Perhaps their sex life had been hobbled by the lie of their secret marriage, or by the Great Crash of '29, which stripped Dad of confidence along with his savings. More likely it was a bad case of repression and inhibition.

We were both virgins when we married. We were terribly ignorant about sex. We knew nothing, Mom explained, as we savored our new intimacy.

What exactly was the problem? I asked.

Poor Sammy got so excited he couldn't keep an erection.

My father, impotent! I could hardly take it in. Never? I asked.

Well, he managed once, she said smiling. He made you.

Early in their marriage, Mom confessed, she tried to learn some curative techniques by taking a doctor for a lover. He was a member of their intimate circle, the Pisha Pasha Club, and an avid sailor. I remember him puffing a pipe in a white captain's hat at the wheel of his boat as our two families went for occasional weekend sails on Lake Erie. (I indulged a secret crush on the doctor's son, who rowed me around in the dinghy.) Mom's affair lasted four years, until the doctor moved his family and practice to Florida. Later, when I was in college, she had another long affair.

Dad's impotence was more shocking to me than Mom's affairs, which I had long suspected and never begrudged, even taking them as license for my own. His was a weakness, hers a strength. Her vivacious sexual style—a combination of flirtatiousness and sweetness that was an integral part of her character—seemed to me a foundation of her power. It was what I studied and adored in her, so that whatever I know in that department I learned at my mother's knee. It was a kind of power many feminists later condemned as a slave's power. But not I. Instead, I chose to use it as a springboard from which to assault the double standard, claiming the same right as men to sexual freedom. (Mom's social lessons did not stop there. As I left my childhood, she counseled me that what you don't admit to can rarely be proved—her personal version of the Fifth Amendment. I realized how adept she was in its use when at age sixty-seven she refused to ride an escalator down to the subway near New York's Museum of Modern Art. I can't, she said, I'm afraid of heights. You? I asked, surprised—since when? All my life, she replied, but I always hid it from you so you wouldn't catch it.)

Whether the doctor's lessons improved Mom's sex life with Dad I'll never know; what went on behind their bedroom door remains a mystery. Since they were always expressing their affection with endearments, caresses, kisses, and doting looks, I suspect they discovered compensations for Dad's impotence. I never once heard them raise their voices to each other or openly quarrel; they seemed devoted to one another. True, in the Shaker house they maintained separate bedrooms, but that was an accommodation to their separate rhythms, which sent Dad, a morning person, to bed by eleven while Mom stayed up half the night reading. A luxurious benefit of excess space, it did not prevent their spending several nights a week together in her bed, Mom told me, until, in their final year in the house when she was wretchedly ill, Dad ignored the round-the-clock aides and insisted on sleeping in her bed every night in case she needed his help. Aside from its apparent sexual limitations, theirs was the marriage I wanted for myself but didn't get till my third and final try.

At Judson, Mom told a story about one member of the

Pisha Pasha Club—a dashing Frenchman named Claude who with his wife Camille had landed in Cleveland in the late 1930s in flight from Hitler. "He was in his eighties when he died, but such a handsome man still. Oh, how the women wept over him at his funeral! Isn't that right, Sam?"

"I presume so," he said wearily.

"You're darn tootin'!" said Mom. "I think each of them thought she was the only one, right up to the day of the funeral," when they discovered from each other that he'd been the lover of many.

Across the room Dad drummed his fingers as Mom continued the story, giggling like a schoolgirl.

"Well, why not?" she retorted to some unspoken challenge. "He brought some European charm into their prosaic lives. Everyone was discreet, so where was the harm? A lot of them were widows by then, anyway."

I remembered Claude bowing to kiss my small hand, could almost hear his low sexy voice, his movie-star French accent. Though he seemed old, I'd thought of him, with his widow's peak and impeccably tailored suits, as Charles Boyer. Had Mom been among the recipients of those vaunted European charms? The delight she took in describing the funeral with Dad right there in the room could be interpreted either way.

Four months after their secret wedding, after Mom's school year was over, they had a family wedding before a rabbi:

The Cleveland News, July 17, 1929: The bride, who was given in marriage by her father, wore pastel green chiffon with matching satin slippers and a picture hat of hair braid. Her bouquet was of yellow roses and lilies of the valley. Miss Jeannette Davis, sister of the bride, sang "At Dawning," preceding the ceremony. The bride's mother, Mrs. Charles Davis, wore black satin and a shoulder corsage of Columbia roses. The groom's mother, Mrs. Harry Kates, was gowned in black chiffon and wore a corsage of Ophelia roses. . . . A wedding tea was given at the home of the bride's parents, following the ceremony at The Temple. Afterward, Mr. Kates and his bride left for a motor trip to Canada

where, though Mom was now forcibly unemployed, they bought two large white stoneware vases, a cloisonné table lamp with a rosette pattern (now lighting my New York loft), and a starter set of Wedgwood dinnerware for six. Upon their return, full of plans, they took up residence in a small apartment on the Heights.

Then suddenly, in October, before Mom had given her first dinner party with their new china, the financial markets, the banks, the businesses that employed my father's clients, the entire world, it seemed, crashed to a halt. Their bank eventually locked its doors, never to reopen. The stylish trousseau on which my mother had burned her savings was rendered obsolete in a season by the sudden precipitous descent of stock prices and hemlines. Like her teaching certificate once she was married—worthless.

They had each come from poverty; now they were back. But so, they consoled each other, was everyone. They, at least, were young: twenty-two and twenty-seven. Mulling over their prospects as they dined on noodles off Wedgwood plates, they decided that since Mom's chances for a job were nil, she might as well improve them by resuming college. As soon as she enrolled in Western Reserve University as an undergraduate history major (history, political science, foreign affairs—these were the subjects she thought crucial in such times), she found a job, marginal but steady, teaching night school English classes to "foreigners," who needed no protection from the corrupting influence of a teacher presumed to engage in marital sex.

Eventually she used her skills to help my grateful Yiddish-speaking grandparents improve their written English. "December 13, 1931. Dear children," wrote Grandma Kates. "Wednesday we were at Dorothys. She gave us the first lesson. That means Mrs Davis, and Pops, and me. And we liked very much her lesson." By then my parents had taken in Bob. "The baby is very nice," Grandma Kates declared, "only he was crying all evening. But at the same time we had there a very good time."

Grandma Davis, who wrote to her children from Miami Beach where her sister Rose and niece Fanny lived, expressed herself, in Davis fashion, more colorfully:

Saturday evining. Dear Dorothy, I am filing fine and I have here a wery good time. Fanny taks Ent Rose and me wery oftin hout far lonch samtime 30 and 40 mils from here to wery swanke plaises. yesterday Fanny tok me an Ent Rose to allewood to see her frends and they leve rit on the atlantig oshen the windes ar nekst to the water and the bots going fort and bek and it is just wonderfool to see. you see so many thinks here that yow cant see in Cleveland. I have 2 big windes in my room so in the front of my windes is pam tres and cocanots on the tres and so many wonderfool thinks that it is well wort to see this and I am glaid I came her. tomora we ar going hot for dinner and efter dinner we will go caling or sit seeng. they ar all very good to me. I have nothing mor to tel yow. I hope yawl not braik all your tit reding this. love and best wishes Mother

As the Depression settled in for the long haul, it began to offer opportunities to middle-class strivers like Mom, on the lookout, and Dad, on the rise. Even as it devastated the country with foreclosures, it glutted the markets with bargain-priced houses and stocks, enabling my parents eventually to take a mortgage on a house for the price of the delinquent taxes and tempting my father to stick another toe in the stock market. By mid-decade it had created the WPA, showpiece of Roosevelt's New Deal, providing jobs for unemployed artists, writers, and scholars, any and all of which Mom aspired to be.

She was on a roll. Marriage, college, two children, a single-family house, and shortly after we moved in, a chance at a creative career. The head of the History Department invited her to work with him as a designer of history projects for the WPA ("Wuppa," as my mother and her colleagues called it). To earn her salary, she needed only to think up and supervise useful research that could be done by unemployed white-collar workers nosing about among the vast records of city, county, and state. A new and open field, a great opportunity, and the money she earned would more than pay for the maid to replace her at home.

So it happened that, unlike other mothers in our neighborhood, most of whom stayed home, my mother dressed up smartly each morning in stockings and pumps, hat and gloves, and drove downtown with Dad to take up her post at a paper-strewn desk alongside dozens of other workers who seemed to me so effervescent and worldly (even though when I came to visit they sometimes took me on their laps and let me try out their typewriters) that I am always shocked to hear the WPA dismissed as "relief," "welfare," "the artist's dole." In the four years she worked there, I went to Mom's office no more than half a dozen times, and then for only the briefest of visits. Yet those few whiffs of her excitement and happiness in that lively office were strong enough to fire my own imagination and ambitions.

Alison Lurie wrote in an essay on Mary McCarthy:

> Before Mary McCarthy, if an educated girl did not simply abdicate all intellectual ambitions and agree to dwindle into a housewife, there seemed to be only two possible roles she could choose: the Wise Virgin and the Romantic Victim. In classical terms, you could opt for Athena or for Psyche. As Athena you would renounce love and marriage and children and become a kind of secular nun. . . . Your life would be calm, productive, admirable—and also . . . a little empty and sad. . . . But suppose you did not want to be either a happy housewife (or, as we used to call it at Radcliffe, "a contented cow") or a dignified spinster? The only alternative seemed to be the role of Psyche, in love with Love. We knew what to expect along this route: you would live intensely, . . . [and] you would suffer. . . . Clearly, there were serious drawbacks to both these roles, not to mention that of domestic cow. But most of us couldn't imagine any alternative until Mary McCarthy appeared on the scene. Her achievement was to invent herself as a totally new type of woman who stood for both sense and sensibility; who was both coolly and professionally intellectual, and frankly passionate,

and who also elected to be a mother.

To my mother, the roles of Wise Virgin, Romantic Victim, and Cow, contented or otherwise, were equally unacceptable. But with the model of Mary McCarthy not yet available, she had to work out her own composite life.

From childhood on, she'd had artistic yearnings. "Our parents were poor people," she recalled, looking lucidly back from her Judson room. "I had only one sweater to wear all through high school, but they gave us education. Singing lessons for Lilian and Jeannette, piano for me and Celia. . . ." Of her six siblings, not one of whom raised children, Jeannette grew up to be a singer; Rosemary and Harry worked in their own commercial art studio; Celia, a Freudian social worker, married Leon, a violinist; and Lilian accomplished the amazing feat of putting herself through law school. Papadear alone, the firstborn, the brooding masher, drinker, and gambling man who left high school to help Grandpa Davis make a living, lacked artistic or intellectual accomplishments.

Beginning in high school, Mom ran with a bohemian crowd of musicians, artists, and dancers, whose recitals we children attended and often tried to mimic, draping ourselves in the dancer's boas and gowns as we waltzed around her attic studio. When Mom joined the WPA, her circle expanded to include a group of dedicated professional women who had more adamantly than she rejected the roles of victim, virgin, and cow. The men in that crowd are a blur compared to the dashing women, many of whom were lesbians, though the term was never spoken in our house.

In particular, my mother's boss, the deep-voiced Mary ("Lefty") Warner, with the powerful stride, broad smile, cropped brown hair she wore slicked straight back into a ducktail, and the kindest eyes I've ever seen, made a powerful and permanent impression on me. She shared a house with her vivacious long-haired lover, Vivian Garrison, and Vivian's two teen-aged children, Dude and Ellen, all glorious rangy redheads. My parents' admiration for Lefty and Vivian filtered through to me, though I was distressed by the fact that Vivian was divorced and her children fatherless, a circumstance more remarkable to me than that two women formed a couple. Like ours, Vivian's family seemed to have some tragic mystery at its core. The frequent parties at their house, where my parents were token straights, excited me with grown-up aspirations. They were animated by witty chatter, passionate debates, loud music, forbidden words, dirty jokes, booze. Except for my doting Davis aunts, Lefty (who, after the war, went on from the WPA to achieve even greater brilliance heading the United Nations relief efforts in Spain) was always my favorite grown-up: when she squatted down to address me eye-to-eye as if I were her equal, I blushed with embarrassed pleasure. I am still grateful for her flattering attentions to me and her patient expectation that I could learn whatever she took the trouble to teach me, including how to strip down to the white bone the delicious meat of the spare ribs she barbecued to a perfect crisp in her fireplace.

When the WPA folded and that crowd dispersed after the war, I listened for news of them, feeling a pang as each one moved away, lost touch, or died. One of them, Ruth Seid, whom my mother had helped find a job, was the novelist Jo Sinclair—the only writer I ever met as a child. Like Lefty, she wore her hair slicked back in a ducktail and revealed deep dimples when she smiled. Knowing that a colleague of my mother wrote books about a Jewish family in Cleveland and women working for the WPA gave me my first inkling that writers were ordinary people like us. At the same time, her books, arranged on our bookshelves alongside the novels of Sinclair Lewis and Upton Sinclair (for both of whom she'd androgynously named herself), made her a person of reach and consequence. Together, my mother and her WPA colleagues gave me a magnified sense of possibility not shared by my classmates. Of possibility, that is, for women, it being understood that however remarkable their accomplishments, they were less significant than those of men.

My father's office, high in the Hippodrome Building, was more exalted and forbidding than Mom's. He sat at a massive oak rolltop desk behind a closed door in a private office with large windows that overlooked the city, conducting important business that must not be interrupted, while I, alone or with Bob, remained outside in the book-lined reception room, drawing pictures at a long table between two secretaries who typed documents and routed calls through an intriguing switchboard. Patiently I drew, touching nothing not mine, trying not to fidget as I waited for the moment when Dad would open his door and invite us in; but usually when the door opened he merely smiled at us and summoned instead one of the secretaries to bring her pad into his office for dictation. Occasionally we were allowed inside to sit quietly by on a leather couch while Dad dictated a letter (Honorable Sir, In reference to yours of the seventeenth . . . , he would say, pacing the carpet, and sometimes, Strike that sentence), after which we would return with the secretary to the reception room to wait again. Behind other closed doors sat other men who also poked their heads out to summon a secretary and smile at us, including my namesake, Alexander B. Cook himself. Just before closing time, Dad would call us inside. While he returned folders to their files and straightened his desk, we were permitted to examine the beguiling compartments beneath the mysterious rolltop, where I was proud to see the blue ceramic bear I'd made for him in school functioning as a paper weight, or take turns twirling on his swivel chair until he donned his hat and coat, rattled closed the rolltop, and locked desk, files, and office for the night.

Not until late adolescence would I aspire to claim for myself the authority that permeated my father's orderly Olympian office, with its leather and glass and oak, audaciously entertaining the prospect of a life of law—and not as secretary, either! Until then, as scissors cut paper, rock breaks scissors, and paper covers rock, it was my enterprising busy mother, with her easy laugh and cluttered desk, her face powder and perfume, pursuing a life of culture, glamour, and pleasure, whom I planned to be when I grew up.

Late each afternoon, after she had changed out of her office clothes into slacks and blouse and started dinner cooking, Mom would light a cigarette, set it in an ashtray on the piano, sit down on the bench, arrange her music, and practice. She played slowly, leaning forward to stare intently at the page, her fingers poised over the keys until her long red nails clicked on the yellowed ivories and the notes poured forth. Sometimes she repeated a phrase a dozen times before she took a long drag on her Chesterfield and moved on to the next one. As she struggled with her Mozart sonatas and Chopin nocturnes, I sat beside her basking in her smell, watching now her fingers, now the score, trying to anticipate when she would suddenly fling up her hand to flip over and slap open the page before dashing back to the keys.

Bob, who reluctantly took piano lessons and hated to practice, refused to join us. Instead, he stretched out in front of the radio to await the coded messages that followed our favorite programs' commercials. At his urgent signal I grabbed a pencil and my secret decoder to join him on the floor, where we competed madly to see who could decode the message first, until Dad, home at six, handed us the funnies (to "share," not "fight over") and a stick each of Wrigley's Spearmint chewing gum, and Mom returned to the kitchen.

The kitchen was an alien place to me; until I married at twenty, the only thing I ever cooked was fudge. Mom never gave me kitchen tips or asked for my help, and I never offered it. My job was to set the table (Bob's was to take out the garbage), which I accomplished with the aid of a tuneful checklist Dad helped me compose as a memory aid. Through the swinging door I carried:

plates, silver, napkins,
water, milk
cups-and-saucers,
salt-and-pepper,
bread, butter, chairs,
cream and suu-uuu-gar.

I also set at Mom's place a small silver bell for summoning the maid—a young Polish, Czech, or Slovenian woman who took care of us after school while Mom was at work and would, as soon as dinner was over and the dishes done, climb to her room on the third floor to tune in her own radio programs. Somehow the bell never made it into the song.

When we were all seated, Mom rang the bell. Then the maid backed through the swinging door bearing serving platters and covered dishes piled with food: pork chops or veal roast or chicken (Bob being allergic to beef and lamb), potatoes mashed or baked or scalloped, a green or yellow vegetable, a bowl of lettuce-and-tomato salad.

Had Johnny and Miss Daisy already eaten in the kitchen? Or were they with us at the table? Search as I may, I cannot find them in this picture, which disturbingly resembles a set scene from an illustrated magazine.

When everyone was served, our parents launched their tantalizing grown-up conversation. At the first expression of interest by one of us children, Dad stopped to explain in dry clear language the intricacies of his latest case or the implications of a court decision. Mom's conversation sparkled more brightly than his, with tales of intrigue and office politics that were, however, harder to follow. If they had urgent private matters to discuss, they resorted to a halting, unfathomable Yiddish. Then Bob and I might launch our own surreptitious conversation, consisting of kicking each other under the table and mouthing insults over it, like a pair of ordinary siblings. Sometimes we filled our mouths with milk and threatened to spray each other, or flaunted wide-open mouths full of chewed-up food, followed by giggling spasms or coughing fits. Our parents, absorbed in their stories, tried to ignore us, but sooner or later Dad succumbed to our provocations. After repeatedly asking us in his modulated voice to stop, eventually he'd lose his patience. For the last time, if you two don't settle down and behave yourselves, you'll have to leave the table. I want you settled by the time I count three. One . . . two . . . Except once, when Dad tucked us each under an arm, tore up the stairs, and threw us down on our beds, leaving me sobbing so hard I couldn't breathe, we always stopped before the fatal three. Or else one of us said, Please may I be excused? Mom was glad to dismiss us as soon as we finished our milk. When we'd wiped our milky lips and tossed our napkins on the table, we'd dash away, leaving our parents to scintillate without us till we returned for dessert.

This cozy prewar dinner scene—whether sheer illusion or, as I grew up believing, repeated in a million middle-class suburban homes—was the model I imagined for my own family. That enchanted memory was one reason I decided at the last minute to abandon my long-standing vow to have no children. But illusions don't work. While my parents managed to keep our dinners going smoothly night after night, year after year, a generation later I could seldom bring it off, no matter how hard I tried. I've often thought about the reasons for the chaos of my table, where half the time the father failed to show and the other half we were so ridden with strife that someone wound up banished in tears. I think it was partly the colliding personnel, partly the drastically altered times, which made the traditional family bargain unacceptable. But it was also in part that seductive, unattainable fantasy that had lodged permanently in my imagination.

*

When I was nine and Bob was ten, World War II descended on our house and everything changed. Uncle Abe remarried and took Johnny back; Miss Daisy was let go; the maid went to work in a war plant; and with the military draft threatening to pluck Dad from us unless Mom gave up that second paycheck, Mom left her job at the WPA.

For a while she continued as an unpaid advisor to certain WPA research programs, and the war itself brought new outlets for her talents and energies: she organized a USO center to entertain the boys, collected blankets and clothing for refugees, mobilized suburban women in support of

FDR's next term. But however high she rose in her ever expanding community-organizing projects—political, cultural, civic, Jewish, women's—she never again had a paying job. Never again did she leave each day for an office to bring tales of intrigue back to the dinner table. Instead, succumbing to the ubiquitous postwar propaganda designed to return women to the home and their paying jobs to demobilized soldiers, my mother, like most middle-class mothers of her generation, embraced the notion that her place was at home with her children.

In later years she claimed that we'd begged her to stop working and stay home with us. I don't remember that—no more than my own children remember imploring me to stay married to their father until they finished high school. I'm not surprised: to the child the request is but one more plea for consideration, while to the mother it carries the unforgettable sting of maternal guilt.

Mom's near contemporary, the poet Virginia Hamilton Adair, who abruptly stopped publishing her work while raising her children, not to resume until her old age, expressed an anxiety about the effect of her work on her children that I believe Mom shared: "They didn't like me for writing. It took time from them. Sometimes . . . I could hear Douglass sort of shooing and shushing the children: 'Now, don't disturb Ginny. She's writing.' And I knew at that moment that they hated me for wanting to write, and I even hated Douglass for shooing them." Secretly torn, she gave up publishing though not writing, as Mom gave up pay though not work.

In Mom's files I found a clipping of an August 22, 1945, *Cleveland News* interview with my thirty-eight-year-old mother, honoring her as three-time president of the Federation of Jewish Women of Greater Cleveland, a confederation of sixty Jewish women's organizations whose presidents met monthly to set policy. Mom headed them all. From the *News* interview I learn that the year I was born, when she was twenty-five, Mom made her first foray into public life by volunteering for the speakers bureau of the Foreign Affairs Council (later the Council on World Affairs). Thirteen years later, at thirty-eight, besides running "Federation," she is sitting on the boards of the Council of Jewish Women, Hadassah, B'nai B'rith Heights Lodge, Women's Action Committee for Lasting Peace, USO Council, President's Round Table of the Woman's Forum, and Cleveland Round Table Conference of Christians and Jews. Her "war activities" include leading a project "serving four overseas Army chaplains, whose itemized needs of morale items for the boys called for shipments averaging 80 pounds weekly." Yet, "son Robert, 13, and his year-younger sister Alix, pupils at Roxboro Junior High, find their mother ready at the drop of a hat to accompany them on a hike."

A hike? I recall no hikes. That's the propaganda showing through. Aside from an occasional night out dancing, Mom was singularly unathletic. Those hikes were invented to demonstrate that no matter how busy, Mom was available to her children "at the drop of a hat." Perhaps it's true. I don't remember and didn't care. She was the one who cared. It was the imperative of the age that motherhood and housework come first. "Through streamlined housekeeping methods and planned once-a-week marketing this busy woman has found time for war activities," wrote the admiring reporter.

I remember well the housekeeping—the countless bags of groceries Mom lugged in from the car; the family wash she hauled up the basement stairs to hang outside on the clothesline, then back down to iron, then up two flights to deposit in our drawers and closets; the daily maintenance tasks of dusting, cooking, mopping, dishes; the weekly "thorough cleaning" when she vacuumed and scrubbed the floors; the seasonal shopping, mending, hemming, moth-proofing. Occasionally, when Dad was feeling flush, Mom hired a weekly cleaning woman to help her out. But it remained her defining role; the rest was extra.

For all her activism, without a paying job Mom's authority at home was subtly undermined, her status gradually diminished, as she assumed the dependent role of *housewife*. Since most of the mothers I knew were housewives, and Mom never complained, I didn't question her comedown, but it settled inside me as a caution. To escape that despised identity was one reason I left Cleveland, and to challenge it one reason I was drawn to feminism. After I quit my own job to have children, I went to extraordinary lengths to avoid having to list *housewife* as my occupation: student, freelance, researcher—anything but that demeaning appellation.

In the photo that accompanies the interview, with her thin penciled eyebrows, dark lipstick, and hair upswept, my mother looks like one of the dark-haired stars pictured in the movie scrapbooks my cousin Marian handed down to me on the day she joined the Marines. Not one of the tough, sultry dames like Joan Crawford, Rita Hayworth, or Barbara Stanwyck, who knew how to wield power, but a tender one with soulful eyes, like Irene Dunne, Joan Fontaine, Norma Shearer, or Laraine Day, whose sweet faces I studied in those scrapbooks precisely to discover their resemblance to my mother. In the clipping Mom's heart-shaped face is framed by a cloud of glamorous fluff arranged on top of her head. She wears a smart wool dress with a V-neckline, and she is as beautiful as any movie star.

Pride puffed me up and lifted me like a kite when I saw her picture in the paper: she was beautiful and accomplished, *and* she was my mother, who came to school like any other mom to confer with my teachers or see me perform. Sitting beside her in the car to go shopping, I savored the moment she turned her torso toward me to check the rear window as she backed out of the driveway. Then the sight of one gloved hand on the steering wheel and one on top of the seat behind my head, the frontal whiff of her perfume and her face powder, the sound of her stockings rubbing against one another as she stretched her short legs toward the gas pedal and clutch filled me with an inarticulate joy that she was mine.

"In my opinion," wrote my father in his memoir, "Dorothy was one of the prettiest girls in town. She is still, at age 82, a lovely-looking woman. And smart too."

There you have it, the judgment of an era: lovely-looking first, smart the afterthought. We all fell for it, as perhaps she wanted. As Bob and I passed into adolescence, her continued activism faded from our regard until she became for us nothing but a mother, whose advocacy and devotion we took increasingly for granted and accepted as our lucky due.

Chapter 7

For more than a decade, ever since my children had graduated from high school leaving me free of responsibility, I'd been spending my long summers alone on an offshore island in Maine in an isolated seaside cabin. There, in uninterrupted solitude, without electricity, phone, plumbing, heat, or road, where often my only conversations were weekly phone calls home from the island's one erratic pay phone, capacities unknown to me in my dense urban life began to flower. As I wrote and reflected in that simple setting, learning to make do with whatever I found around me—the wild greens, seaweeds, and shellfish I gathered for my meals, the slow dialogue of letters—the independence I'd been unsuccessfully cultivating since I'd left my parents at twenty finally came to fruition. The surprising self-reliance I learned on that island had so expanded my life that I devoted my last book, *Drinking the Rain,* to extolling it.

But now, with my parents in ever imminent crisis, that precious isolation began to seem a liability. It was one thing to free yourself of dependence on others but quite another to find others dependent on you. As I had once been for my children, now I was my parents' main support.

Without a phone in my cabin to maintain our contact

or receive the dire emergency call, dependent on infrequent ferries to get me near an airport, I learned the precariousness of independence, the limits of self-reliance. Soon my daily goal was to find a way to telephone Judson. When the pay phone was broken, I humbly beggared myself to impose on my neighbors.

To my surprise, rather than resenting the interruption of my solitude, I relished being needed. In the scales of fulfillment, devotion may sometimes outweigh freedom. Years had passed since my children had needed me, leaving a hole I had eagerly crammed with selfish satisfactions but now filled with my parents' needs. Not that they asked my help; scrupulously they asked nothing. But with our power reversed, I no longer feared being swamped by love. The greater their dependency, the more unstintingly I gave myself—not out of virtue but out of feeling.

I had uncovered this capacity in myself several years before, when my husband had suddenly collapsed with an aneurysm. As I slowly nursed him back to health, instead of feeling burdened, as I would have expected, I felt my commitment swell. The barriers to our intimacy, which I had erected in the name of independence, fell away, revealing behind them at the crossroads of the selfish and the selfless a person who basked in the powers of devotion despite the upheaval of my life. Now once again, as I discharged my duties, I found myself savoring their delights, not least of which was the sweet caress of my parents' gratitude.

*

One misty day, after I'd run across the long beach to phone Judson from a neighbor's house, Dad announced with great excitement, "I think I'm going to win a million dollars."

"Really!" I said, catching his excitement. "What makes you think so?"

He hesitated. "I just think so."

"Why?"

"They sent me a letter. My name is listed as a sweepstakes winner."

I was suspicious. Hadn't we all received such announcements emblazoned with our names and promptly tossed them in the trash? Yet, knowing my cautious father to be the last man on earth to be taken in by a notorious scam, I allowed myself a moment of hope as I asked, "Are you sure, Daddy? Who sent it?"

"*Time* magazine. All I have to do is fill out and submit certain forms."

"Do you have to send them money?"

"No, but I thought it wouldn't hurt to subscribe."

My hopes sank. Dad would never have subscribed to *Time* if he hadn't been duped. All through my childhood the *Ladies' Home Journal, Saturday Evening Post, Reader's Digest, National Geographic,* and assorted other journals arrived in the mail weekly or monthly—not because we wanted them but because Dad could not refuse Mr. Joseph Cavaliero, the gentleman in black suit, necktie, black hat, and two metal leg braces who dragged and pivoted himself up our front walk twice a year to sell subscriptions. Not even Mr. Cavaliero could sell Dad *Time.* When our social studies teachers required that each student subscribe to a weekly news magazine (*Time* and *Newsweek* were recommended), Dad proposed I take the *Nation* or the *New Republic.* At home we took the muckraking newsletter *In Fact,* the radical daily *PM,* and the slicker weekly *Reporter* until each of them folded. Never *Time.*

Instead of protesting, I calmly asked Dad to mail me a copy of the announcement. By the time it arrived in Maine, revealing in the microscopic *if*-clause that after sending in the forms Dad would merely become eligible for a future drawing with the same long odds as any lottery, he had already sent out gifts of thousands of dollars each to his sister, his grandchildren, his great-grandchildren, and to me.

Did this magnanimous gesture mark the onset of Dad's cerebral decline? What but the dotage of age could have induced a lifelong devotee of the fine print—a superskeptical rationalist whose judgment was so highly esteemed that for half a century he had been sought as an independent arbitrator in labor-management disputes all over the country—to rashly ignore the crucial *if* and succumb to fantasy? What but delusion could persuade this most cautious of spenders, for whom each penny had always glinted a bit like gold, to jettison a lifetime's frugality and give away his carefully accumulated savings like so many Chiclets? Was this the same man who, when Mom was moved from their apartment to nursing care, had been so worried about the increased expense that he'd drafted letters to the many recipients of his ongoing birthday checks—his grandchildren and great-grandchildren, grandnieces and -nephews— explaining that due to a sudden change in circumstances, he would no longer be sending out the annual gifts (until Mom, learning of the letters, had shamed him into tearing them up)? Now he had sent out gifts hundreds of times larger and insisted we keep them. It was not that he'd lost touch with reality but only that his shrinking reality now excluded the fine print.

For a while I kept on thanking him—for myself and my children. I made a special point to mention each generous act I could remember—from his current contributions to his sister's rent, the car he bought his grandson in graduate school, the legal help he provided the extended family, to the excess insurance he purchased from Bob to help him reach a certain goal, and on back to their taking in

Grandma Davis after she was widowed, and our college educations, and their investments in each enterprising relative's retail ventures, and their sheltering Johnny until Uncle Abe remarried. . . .

At this point in my recitation, Dad added something that shocked me: "And we took in Bob, you know."

I remembered a conversation I'd had with Mom a decade earlier, when she first began confiding her secrets. We were speaking at last of the long affair she'd had with a man I'll call Kenneth when I was in college, an affair I didn't begin to figure out until my thirties, when I was trying to write a novel about those days.

When you were in love with Kenneth, why didn't you and Daddy split up? I'd asked her.

Why would we? I'm not sure Sam was ever even aware of it, she said.

You never told him?

Oh, no!

But don't you think he must have known?

He may have known unconsciously that something was different. But in those days he was so wrapped up in his work and often out of town on hearings. If he did know, he never said anything about it—though he did try extra hard to please me then.

Like how?

Well, for example, by agreeing to buy this house.

So that was why he agreed! It finally made sense to me. Well then, I asked, what about you? Didn't you ever think of leaving him?

She did a double take. Why no, she said, I never even considered it.

Why not?

Why would I? I loved Sammy and our life together. We

were family. And he was always very good to me. Why, even if the idea had crossed my mind I would not have acted on it because I was so grateful to him for raising Bob.

Grateful? I was astonished. I couldn't imagine what *grateful* meant in such a context. That raising Bob was her job, not his? Or that it was a burden to be borne? Or that it was finally a question of genes after all, since genetically Bob was a Davis but not a Kates.

The importance of genes had become one of my running disagreements with Dad. Once, after I'd sent him a book by Stephen Jay Gould arguing against the inheritance of IQ, he called me long-distance, which he considered an extravagance, to ask, Let me get this straight—are you telling me you believe that traits like intelligence and temperament are not carried in the genes? Is that what you believe? Yes, Daddy, I said, I believe everyone is born with intelligence and the possibility of the whole range of temperamental response. The difference is a matter of nurture. So, he replied, so. I just wanted to make sure.

But if genes were so important to Dad, then what of Bob's children, whom he adored? And Bob's children's children, Dad's great-grandchildren, who delighted him in his old age?

I can't understand, I said to Mom, feeling the beginnings of exasperation, why you would feel *grateful.* Bob was just as much Dad's son as yours, wasn't he?

Yes, she conceded, he was Sam's son too. But, she added after a long pause, there was all the expense involved.

What could expense have to do with it? I'd concluded that her odd idea that Dad deserved *gratitude* for raising his own son must be some private madness of hers. And now here was Dad sitting in his Judson apartment speaking of Bob's adoption as of some benevolent act of charity, confirming Mom's disturbing intuition.

There are many things for which a parent may want gratitude that a child takes for granted. And heading the list is life itself. Next comes anything the parent gives easily, without a qualm. After that, it's whatever the child must win by fighting, cajoling, whining, begging—for which the parent earns not gratitude but resentment. No wonder that honoring thy father and thy mother requires a commandment from God!

As sole breadwinner in our family and vigilant keeper of the books, Dad calculated the price of everything. I can still hear his anxious words, *Think of the expense!* echoing through my childhood. Not that money was his ultimate standard. Honesty ranked higher than frugality in his pantheon of virtues; no sum could ever tempt him from it. "As an arbitrator, no one in my more than forty years in that capacity ever tried to bribe or corrupt me," he wrote in his memoir. "I know that any such effort would have been swiftly repulsed." The stories of his childhood handed down to us by Grandma Kates often involved the return of money: a dollar discovered on the sidewalk to the police, a gold coin received on his paper route to its unwitting donor. He was so upright that he once lectured me for taking a small airline pillow for one of my babies to sleep on and considered an overdue library book or late payment of a bill a kind of theft. At the culmination of sixty-five years of practicing law, his charge for a day was what other lawyers charged for an hour. "Your father didn't seem to be interested in money like other lawyers but simply loved the law," said his former neighbor, Peter Coles, husband of the Canadian ambassador to Portugal, who had phoned me to report on his visit to Judson.

"Were you shocked when you saw them?" I asked.

"Yes, quite shocked," he confessed, "especially by your mother, though she did recognize me, and I got her to remember the children. But your father and I had a very good conversation. I kept thinking of a line from St. Thomas Aquinas: 'Whatever is right ought to be law, and whatever is law ought to be right.' Sam followed that ought principle all his life. My friends and I agree that if we ever have to be judged we'd like to be judged by Sam Kates."

As the object of his frequent judgment, I couldn't disagree. In meting out justice Dad was dispassionate and lenient, so that whatever my punishment I usually considered myself lucky to have my behavior examined according to the highest principles, unlike my friends, who got spanked and yelled at—though who wouldn't prefer not to be judged at all? Peter Coles also spoke of Dad's generosity, recalling that whenever Dad played chess with Peter's two young sons he'd send them each home with a dollar bill. "I think my Nicholas developed his love of chess from Sam and those dollars," he said to me.

In my childhood, it was in dimes and quarters, raisins and chewing gum, that Dad rewarded virtue. Yet as willing as he was to dispense cash, he was loath to condone what we spent it on, thus undermining his own generosity. Even Mom had to justify her purchases, despite Dad's palpable delight in their fruits. Not that he denied her what she wanted, either for herself or for her children—she wouldn't have stood for it—but as our chief fiduciary officer with a powerful pocket veto, he tried to dampen our desires, making us plead, connive, or justify, until, with a final beleaguered Bumstead sigh of capitulation, he yielded.

Mom's generosity, which kept her ever our advocate, was second nature to her (for which we rewarded her by taking it for granted); Dad's, tempered by the insecurity and thrift born of immigrant poverty and Depression marriage, was a trait he had to cultivate in himself like good posture. As we wrested concessions from him item by item, our gratitude came to be increasingly grudging—as grudging as the hard-won permission it acknowledged.

I was never sure if it was the principle or the expense he disapproved of. The idea or the money. He invariably registered an objection by word or frown to each of Mom's careful purchases—an elegant dress picked up on sale, the gloves, stockings, and underthings that kept needing to be replenished, the perfumes and cosmetics that kept her glamorous—yet he bowed before the mysteries of her sensuous femininity and enjoyed the swath she cut in the world. How volubly he admired her shapely ankles and calves that rose above her elegant 7AAA pumps. How tenderly he straightened her silk scarf, held her coat for her, stroked her expensively coiffed hair. It was the act of purchase that pained him, not, evidently, the purchases. He was grateful enough to have her take charge of his own questionable wardrobe. Not that he was less than meticulous in his personal habits, twice daily cleaning his fingernails, stopping every week for a shoeshine in the Terminal Tower, smelling always of soap, Listerine, and witch hazel. But buying clothes was difficult. His color blindness accounted for the mismatched socks, but what weakness could explain the occasional frayed collar or shiny seat? Not a shortage of cash, for whatever his misgivings, Mom charged freely to her charge accounts, and he promptly paid the bills. But if not the money, it had to be the principle.

What principle? *Economy and thrift.* For their own sake and at any cost, which sometimes seemed to mean: *buy nothing at all.*

Yet—not nothing. Only no thing. There were items of prudent investment—bonds, insurance, savings certificates, sound stocks—that commanded the same respect from him as did beautiful things from Mom. In our annual negotiations of our allowances, he always allotted a sum to enable Bob and me to buy U.S. Savings Stamps, sold weekly in our classrooms to be pasted into books, which we could eventually trade in for Defense Bonds (later renamed War Bonds) for deposit in his bank vault for safekeeping— where mine remained, earning a modest interest, until my own children were nearly grown.

Among Dad's papers I uncovered a projection of his "Desired Total Worth" from $700 at the age of twenty, when the projection was calculated, to the grand sum of $100,000 at the distant age of fifty, an increase resulting from nothing more than annually compounding a 5 percent return on the original $700 investment. Another document he wrote around the same time is entitled, "Rules for a Long Pull Trader," with the first rule, "Be patient—do not buy in a hurry." A table from a few years later, composed when he was twenty-seven, lists his "Actual Total Worth" by year and quarter, back to age twenty. The sums are somewhat lower than the earlier "Desired" projection but nonetheless steadily increase until 1928 when, as Dad explains in a note, he "lost $1500 selling short American Can Company and spent $1200 on engagement ring and piano." Evidently impatient with a 5 percent return in those wildly speculative days of the late 1920s, when every other clerk invested in the booming stock market, he tried to jump-start his fortune. As he humbly explained in his memoir six decades later, "I began to read financial writings, and mistakenly came to believe that I knew all about stock market cycles and that I could predict them. In my arrogance, I decided in 1927 that the bull market of the 1920s had reached a peak (which in fact occurred two years later). Stocks could then be sold short on a ten percent margin. . . . As the price of the stock which I had sold short rose, I was called to provide more margin, and when I no longer could, my account was liquidated. I have never sold stocks short since."

Stung by the Crash of '29, Dad rerouted his faith to conservative investments and defensive strategies, which became his lifelong habit. I was talking to him on an island neighbor's phone when he announced to me that at the age of ninety-three he had just bought a million-dollar liability insurance policy.

With the house and car about to be sold, I was astounded. "Why in the world would you do that, Daddy?"

"In case I cause an accident and someone sues me."

Though other residents made way for him as he pushed his walker down the ramp to Fisher Dining Room, by then he was hardly the dangerous missile he'd once been, cruising the world as Speedy Sam—or, in the words of Alexander B. Cook reported in Dad's memoir, "rushing around like a fart in a gale."

"At Judson? Are you kidding?"

"It's possible," he said.

"Judson must have its own liability insurance," I pointed out. "And anyway, you don't have a million dollars to protect."

His voice was weak, but I could almost see him shake his finger in the air as he proclaimed, "I believe in insurance!"

With a family to raise, a life to create, and no income of her own, Mom had no choice but to pit her desires against Dad's principles. I see this now as the basic conflict of our otherwise tranquil household, the quiet struggle that I spent the rest of my life waging inside myself, favoring now one side, now the other. Fleeing their house, their city, their opinions and approval did nothing to silence it. In my long second marriage the roles were reversed: I was the adamant saver, my husband the easy spender; yet I remember the gleeful triumph I felt when in 1967, as a fledgling feminist with no income of my own, I wrote a check on our joint bank account to benefit the women's liberation movement, perceived by my husband as subversive. It was my mother's triumph I felt; and my slow burn over my husband's control of the purse—a burn that fired the pages of my early feminist article, "A Marriage Agreement"—came from the torch my mother passed to me.

In that article I proposed to divide the tasks of childcare and housework equally between husband and wife—at the time an idea so controversial as to merit a six-page spread in *Life,* more than two thousand letters from *Redbook* readers, and attacks by Norman Mailer and the *New York Times.* Its first principle read: "We reject the notion that the work which brings in more money is more valuable. The ability to earn more money is a privilege which must not be compounded by enabling the larger earner to buy out of his/her duties." Employing the rational tools of my father to defend the position of my mother.

Many years later I was astonished to read in Dad's sister Eva's memoir of her childhood that Dad had anticipated my agreement by nearly fifty years: To settle the ongoing arguments over dishwashing tasks between Eva and another sister, Sophie, "Sam's legal mind came to the rescue. He was already in law school, so he drew up a contract specifying certain dishwashing days for each of us. Very seriously, we signed that contract which was duly witnessed by a friend of Sam's, and our quarrels ceased."

. . . .

For a while the rationing and shortages of the war muted my parents' struggle over things. But when the war ended in a national orgy of consumption, their disparate desires resurfaced. As they lay together in their marital bed on Ashurst Road, the hard-won Total Worth required to insure his sleep was subverted by the intangible objects of her dreams—now increasingly embodied in the tangible things that money could buy.

Not that she was, as he seemed to imply, rash or spendthrift. Even after succumbing to the postwar frenzy to return women to the kitchen, Mom worked hard for what she got, frugally cutting corners to conserve her household allowance, striking clever deals, trading up, ferreting out bargains. A careful, prudent shopper, she usually waited for the sales before buying, even switched her cigarette brand for the coupons. In some ways she was Dad's best student in frugality (at least till I came along) and as the more practiced shopper could probably have taught him a trick or two. But though he had the wit to admire her taste and seldom used the veto he kept jangling in his pocket like a ring of keys, such expertise did not interest him.

Too bad. He might have been proud of her successes instead of obliging her to hide the wrapped purchases in a closet until she judged it the right moment to bring them out; he might have made distinctions, approving of some things, disapproving of others. Instead, he always put us through our paces. If an item was full price, he winced at the sum; if it was marked down, his satisfaction was compromised by the inevitable "Final Sale" stamped on the receipt. When Bob pestered him for new football gear or I modeled my back-to-school wardrobe with a stylish twirl, he said he didn't see why we couldn't make do with last year's model. Bob responded with a pained *Oh, Daddy!* and

I submitted an oral brief, dickering until Mom had had enough. *You* may not see why, Sam, but *I* do, she concluded decisively. Next case.

His real objection was not to how we shopped but that we shopped. To him, things themselves were essentially frivolous, their pursuit a problem less of money than of "values." This he'd already decided by age twenty-five when, with the stilted diction of an autodidact who has just downed a strong dose of John Stuart Mill, he assessed his options for a purposeful life in a neatly typed document preserved for seven decades among his private papers. The striking combination of youthful idealism and precocious prudence embodied in its calculations never left him; indeed, the patterns of mind it displays would—diction aside—one day pass to me.

Which ought I to do—concentrate almost solely on attaining what is regarded as professional and financial success, or ought I, rather, apply myself to my profession during the normal working hours only, spending the remainder of my time in pursuits unconnected to it? . . .

If I should concentrate on "success," I would become too occupied with matters pertaining to advancement to be troubled by the misery or sufferings of others . . . and incapable of enjoyable association with cultured minds. . . .

On the other hand, if I should restrict my work to a portion of my waking hours, the remainder of my time to be spent in developing myself culturally, esthetically, mentally, and socially; . . . if I should seek constantly to slake my curiosity in whichever direction it should take itself; if I should adhere to the ideals of justice and the dictates of conscience; it seems to me that my life would be more enjoyable than if I were to make mere "success" my ultimate purpose. . . .

It is true that at times I should probably be sorry to be regarded as a failure by those expecting great things of me. But would not these periods of depression be more than counterbalanced by my enjoyment of a life devoted to beauty and art and cultural pursuits, to the search for truth, to conduct in harmony with good conscience, and to an endeavor to obtain the greatest net happiness in life?

Around the time he composed this document, he began courting Mom. Even at twenty she seemed to him the ideal usher into that lofty world of beauty, art, culture, and truth he feared himself too narrowly focused to penetrate on his own. ("Dorothy has had an important influence on my life. Among other things, she awoke my love for music. We have been regular symphony goers ever since our marriage. Among our friends are four composers and several concert pianists and violinists," he saw fit to record in his brief memoir.)

In 1926, before falling in love, he had bought his first car, a used Model A Ford; after becoming engaged to Mom the following year, he traded it in for a new grey two-door Chevrolet coupé that he taught his fiancée to drive. "The very first time Dorothy drove it without me, she managed to dent a fender," he lamented. But never mind. Soon he was using his savings on a diamond engagement ring and a piano for his beloved. Dad's sister told him that Mom was a "gold-digger" (for which Mom never forgave her)—a charge Dad dispatched by trying to educate Mom to care less about things, as she tried to tutor him to care more.

How it must have alarmed him to see her champion my own increasingly extravagant desires for each season's imperative new clothes: for the right shade of penny loafer, for cashmere sweater sets and matching skirts, for my confirmation pink-gold ruby cocktail ring, for a sweet-sixteen monogrammed silver cigarette case, for a beaver coat for graduation—and all by appeal to that adamant arbiter, *everyone else.*

This fiction so disgusted him that his brow furrowed like a washboard whenever we invoked it. Everyone else? he jibed, visibly pained that we should submit our desires to so mindless a court. He happened to know several people in our very school—our cousins, for instance—who needed no such things and couldn't afford them if they did. He never understood that theirs was the fate we shopped to avoid. While we waited him out, Dad protested, admonished, suffered, until, with a sigh of resignation, he shook his head and paid the bills.

I hated to see him suffer on my account. I loved him as much as I loved my mother and admired him more, knew that he too, with his superior values, was on my side in a different way. I wanted to warrant his faith that one day I would rise above my wrongheaded longings, drop my frivolous desires, strip down, and, like brave Prince Hal, switch to the side of virtue.

But not yet. Please not yet.

ii | Sweet Sin

I lusted to thieve, and did it, compelled by no hunger, nor

poverty. . . . If ought of those pears came within my mouth,

what sweetened it was the sin.

— SAINT AUGUSTINE, *Confessions*

Me in a cashmere sweater, 1949

Chapter 8

Looking back from Judson to the time when my parents' present dependency was inconceivable, I regretted that our struggle was finished. The reversal of power I tasted each time we spoke was bittersweet. Even as an adolescent I'd savored our invigorating battles—particularly the unforgettable night my father and I wrestled for ascendancy in the foyer of the Ashurst house.

Forbidden to leave the house, in a spurt of defiance I was rushing the front door when he stopped me. With his jaw set, arms spread across the door, he asked, Where do you think you're going?

Out.

No you're not.

After a volley of words and arguments I tried to lunge past him. He stood fast. And then we were suddenly in an unbreakable clinch, twisting, striving, grunting, struggling with all our might for control of the door.

At last, exhausted, we realized we had reached an impasse. Dad, red-faced and panting, dropped his arms, and I retreated to my room. Ostensibly he had won since I stayed in the house, but we both knew that next time I would win.

I also knew my victory would be sour if it ended the frisson of our stimulating struggle. We never wrestled again.

*

Cashmere sweaters being the key to social success in our high school, and given my father's unyielding attitude toward excess purchases, I felt myself gradually being sucked toward the swamp of crime.

Theft was not totally outside my ken. Back in junior high I'd been initiated into a club whose sole purpose was to prey on Woolworth's by the bagful. Despite pressure to perform, after two reluctant forays I quit, recognizing even at twelve the folly of stealing-for-stealing's-sake. Not that I flaunted my virtue, like certain prudes who self-righteously renounced all vice (smoking, drinking, kissing) before ever being tempted; but I wanted to save my transgressions for objects worth the risk. Just so, in the 1960s, charged with civil disobedience, I went to great lengths to avoid conviction, hoping to save my fingerprints and guilty plea for some politically worthy future crime.

There were three basic styles of cashmeres, in ascending order of price, varying only by color: short-sleeved pullovers, long-sleeved pullovers, and long-sleeved cardigans with flat pearl buttons from neck to waist. They were identical in shape, knit, neckline, cuff, and since they were supplied exclusively by two Scottish manufacturers, Hadley and Pringle, who added only a few new colors each year, the way to improve one's collection was by accretion. Combining a short-sleeved pullover with a same-colored cardigan to produce a twin set was as high as you could go within the three basic styles; but there was one thing higher: a "dressmaker cashmere," sporting some unexpected detail (a little edged collar, a V-neck, a discrete breast pocket) and an elevated price to match. As a single dressmaker cashmere could distinguish a modest wardrobe like mine, naturally, that was what I wanted.

Now it happened that my Aunt Rosemary—who'd moved back to our grandparents' house from Pittsburgh after her husband, my dashing Uncle Ray, put a bullet through his head—had assembled a highly personal collection of choice dressmaker cashmeres in styles and makes unavailable in all of Cleveland. She bought them in New York City where, as head buyer of ladies' wear for the Cleveland branch of the May Company, she got to do her personal as well as professional shopping. Often when the Davises partied at our grandparents' house, after dinner I would take my homework upstairs to Aunt Rosemary's room, open the dresser drawer where her sweaters lay wrapped in tissue paper, unwrap them one at a time, and try them on. It was inevitable that one day—perhaps on the eve of a dance—I would slip one into my school bag.

When the inevitable happened, I did not consider it a theft but rather a loan, to be repaid on my next visit to Grandma's house, when I could exchange the sweater for another. My aunt had so many that I doubted she would notice. Getting it out of the house presented no problem— far easier than tiptoeing into my parents' bedroom in the early morning while they slept to brazenly lift a tenner from Dad's wallet, which he trustingly left on top of his dresser alongside his glasses, nail file, keys, hankie, and breath-freshening Sen-Sen. No, the problem was that Aunt Rosemary's sweaters didn't fit. She was a petite small; I was a medium. I decided to solve that problem by stretching them. In a teen magazine I had read that one could ensure against shrinkage while a sweater dried by rolling it in a towel, then pinning it to a pattern made of heavy butcher paper. I made a pattern by tracing one of my own sweaters. But when I pinned onto it Aunt Rosemary's wet bone-colored short-sleeved pullover with a delicate cable stripe, the pins left indelible rust marks, ruining it for us both.

Fearful and penitent, I hid the sweater in my bottom drawer until I could permanently dispose of it and quickly abandoned the project.

Some months later, my immoderate lust for cashmeres was rekindled when Mom came up with a scheme. Darling, she said one evening when Bob was out, come into the study for a moment. I have a proposition to discuss with you.

A proposition? I liked the sound of it. What could it be? Mom seldom asked anything of me. She was all give, no take, when it came to her children, wanting fiercely to equip us with every grace and skill that might advance our social standing and augment our powers. Besides our violin and piano lessons, for which she relinquished to us her piano (as later she would lend us the family car), she overrode Dad's vetoes to offer us acting, sketching, and ballroom dancing classes at, respectively, the Cleveland Play House, the Cleveland Museum of Art, and Florence Shapiro's Dancing School. When our friends stopped by the house to visit at any time of day or night, she immediately made herself scarce, taking Dad upstairs with her. If a prom was in the offing, she considered a new dress for me and a corsage for Bob's date imperative. Otherwise, she stayed discreetly out of our social lives, seldom inquiring where we had gone, though she was obviously bursting to know. She kept snacks on hand for teen refreshment, and if either of us scheduled a meeting or party or sleepover at home, she lavishly stocked the larder, then arranged to be out.

When we were seated in the study behind closed doors, she lit a cigarette, took several thoughtful puffs, and began: Dearest, I know how important your sorority is to you. And what a difference it's made to your social life.

She was right. For those of us who belonged, our sororities, along with the fraternities from which we drew our boys, meant everything. Though Dad condemned their exclusivity and pettiness, joining one had produced enough confidence in me to transform this uncertain outsider into someone who had seventeen friends, who knew how to dance and flirt and kiss and in extremis write out speeches for myself or my sisters to deliver by phone to hapless boys. Like Dad, I'd grown into someone with goals and plans, though not ones he would approve of.

Mom took another drag on her cigarette and examined my face, hesitatingly searching for words before coming out with it. You know, dear, she said, if Bob could get into a fraternity it would mean so much to him. And do so much for him. Just as it's done for you. Don't you think?

Actually I'd never thought of it. Bob in a fraternity? Bob was simply my brother and adversary, not an object of my speculation. Now, with Mom consulting me about him, as if he were our mutual problem, I quickly considered his social plight and, finding it pathetic, wanted nothing to do with it. But I said to her uncertainly, I suppose so.

I knew you would, she said, which brings me to my proposition. She sat back and puffed deeply before continuing. You have a lot of friends in Gammas. It's obvious that they like you very much. I'm sure if you used your influence, asked one or two of them—maybe Lenny or Jack or Arty—to put Bob up for Gammas, it might give him the chance he needs. That's all I'm asking for him, just a chance. Everyone deserves a chance. If he doesn't make it, well at least we did our best. Do you think you could do this for your brother?

I didn't know what to say. Was such a move honorable in our crowd? If word of it got out, could it harm me? If I tried to get my brother in and failed, would it be my failure too? Would his unworthiness rub off on me? If we'd both been boys or both girls, there would be no problem: same-sex siblings were considered "legacies" and automatically accepted (although it was usually the younger, not the elder, who reaped the benefit). But he was a boy, and I had no power to influence boys; all I could do was ask a special favor, which could make me vulnerable. It was a dangerous game. Was I my brother's keeper? No, I decided, I would be too uncomfortable asking this—yet how could I refuse our mother, who, as she leaned forward anxiously awaiting my answer with one hand balling her handkerchief, the other clutching her cigarette, was suffering an even worse discomfort? She asked so little of me. And she was right: getting in could make a tremendous difference to Bob—as great as it had to me. If some Gamma blackballed him, he'd be no worse off than before; but if they took him in, it would make Mom so happy.

If you do this for Bob, said Mom, I'll buy you a new cashmere sweater in any style you like. But you must never tell anyone. Bob must never know you did this or that I asked you to.

Hearing the offer, I suddenly felt stricken with guilt for having reduced her to this. Was I so selfish, so thoughtless, so hard-hearted that she had to bribe me with a sweater? Why had I never thought of trying to help Bob on my own? What kind of sister was I? What kind of person?

At the same time, I felt put upon and ashamed—for Mom and myself. Dad had not been above resorting to rewards to get us to do what he considered important for our characters and futures, like raising our grades; but hearing Mom use the same tactic made me squirm. This wasn't a reward, it was a bribe. My callousness had forced Mom to bribery, and I was so corrupt as to accept it.

Okay, I said, I'll try. But don't count on it. I don't have nearly the influence you think.

She reached over, squeezed my hand, and said, I knew you'd understand. I'll always be grateful to you for this. Bob would be too if he knew. But he must never know—agreed?

Yes, but what if it doesn't work? I asked.

Oh, that's all right. All I ask is that you try your best. You'll get the sweater either way.

I got my reward, a long-sleeved raspberry pullover (that I paired up with a pale pink-and-blue Botany plaid box-pleated skirt), and Bob became a Gamma which, as Mom predicted, improved his life, and until this moment their connection remained a secret between me, myself, and Mom. But addiction is notoriously insatiable, and another season had begun in the department stores. The clothing allowance I now negotiated with Dad every fall on the basis of a written budget seemed inadequate before I had made a single purchase, and my Saturday sales job that would augment it was still in the future.

My girlfriend Gloria told me about a new item in Halle's sweater department: lamb's wool sweaters from England that looked exactly like cashmeres but were half the price. Same styles, shapes, colors—in fact, identical to cashmeres in every way but for the feel and the cost. The next time we went downtown shopping together after school, in the dressing room I hit on a plan. I would charge a lamb's wool sweater on my charge card, then take it and its cashmere look-alike into the dressing room, switch the two price tags, and, leaving the lamb's wool behind, proceed to the elevator with the cashmere in my package. I selected a pair of blue short-sleeved pullovers that looked exactly alike, certain that if I, an expert, couldn't tell one from the other with the naked eye, the scam was foolproof.

Gloria, usually game for anything I proposed, disagreed. When she couldn't dissuade me, she left me on my own to do the switch, offering to wait downstairs till I was finished.

Now it seems to me obvious that it couldn't have worked. The salesclerks, who sold sweaters all day long, were no less expert than I. Yet when I entered the elevator on the third floor, package in hand, and rode down alone, with youthful arrogance I thought I had pulled it off. Puffed with triumph, I found Gloria sampling perfumes. Not until we proceeded through the exit door to be met outside by a waiting security guard did I realize my folly.

What I don't understand, said the manager, examining the Charge-a-Plate with my signature on the back, is why you would want to steal a sweater when you were perfectly able to charge it. It doesn't make any sense to me.

Even if I hadn't been too choked up to speak, how could I explain the arcane politics of money in our family? What stranger could understand that it was out of deep respect for my father that I stole, in order to spare him the disappointment of another painful encounter with the insatiably venal character I shared with Mom. At the thought of my father's disappointment, I dissolved in another round of sobs.

The manager reached over her desk to offer me a tissue. When I had blown my nose, she picked up the phone and said, Now I'm going to call your parents. What's your phone number?

My mother's or my father's? I asked.

Which one would you like me to call?

Which one? The manager was asking *me* to decide which heart to stab in order to be saved? Dumbfounded, I stared at her. Like certain children of divorce pressed to take a side, I was absolutely unable to choose.

Yet I had to choose. Any second I would have to commit the most difficult act of my fifteen years of life and select one of my unsuspecting parents to receive the crushing news of my having stolen and been caught, knowledge I suddenly realized (why hadn't I seen it before?) would break them.

As the manager waited, I pictured my parents in their last moment of innocence before the call. Mom, just starting dinner, or perhaps already on her way upstairs to freshen up. Dad, seated at his desk bent over a lawbook deep in contemplation of justice. Both oblivious of what was coming.

The manager cradled the phone against her shoulder, her finger on the cutoff bar. Well? she said.

Which one? If my mother were called, she would defend and comfort me with boundless understanding. To the manager's charge she would respond, *Oh, no, madame, it must be someone else, I'm sure you're mistaken!* until, confronted with the irrefutable evidence, she would assume the blame herself, searching for all the ways she had let me down. And after blame, grief. How could I do this to my mother?

My father, then, for whom theft was unthinkable, whom I shamed with my mere desires? Must my upstanding, law-revering, high-minded father—whose partner was a former judge!—be humiliated and dishonored by my recklessness? Having betrayed him by stealing, must I betray him again by disgracing him before the manager? No, not my father either, who would never understand.

It was impossible. I could not choose.

The manager waited, finger poised to dial. Well? she repeated, beginning to lose patience.

This was the worst moment of my brief life. I had taken risks before—had cut school, forged my parents' signatures, cheated on tests, tampered with the schedules in the school office to arrange for myself and a girlfriend the equivalent in study halls of triple lunch (time enough to cross the forbidden ravine to Shaker Square to try on the new full-skirted, puff-sleeved spring dresses of striped chintz and polished poplin at Franklin Simon and still be back in time for seventh-period social studies), filched tens and twenties from my father's wallet and that cashmere sweater from Aunt Rosemary's drawer, schemed, shirked, lied, connived, and dragged my reluctant friends along with me—but not until today did I commit the inexcusable blunder of being caught. Nor till this moment did I understand the price: a deathblow to my parents' hearts. No matter which one heard first, both would be undone: Dad by shame, Mom by remorse.

Finally I chose Dad to take the blow. A lawyer and man of the world, he would know how to rescue me (for the first of many times) and could get here in under five minutes.

My father, I said. And with a mix of terror and relief, I gave the manager his office number.

About a week into my provisional three-month grounding (the longest of my life, for which Dad had kindly supplied me with *Don Quixote, Tristram Shandy,* and *The Red and the Black*), Mom said gravely, I thought you would want to know that I've been to see a psychiatrist about you.

A psychiatrist! As if I were mad instead of bad. On top of having brought my father to tears (in front of the manager!), and all the other suffering I'd caused, I'd driven Mom to a psychiatrist, whose bill Dad would now have to foot on top of Bob's allergy and reading specialists'.

What did you tell him? I asked. What did he say?

He was recommended to me by Celia, said Mom. Aunt Celia, brainiest of my Davis aunts, was a psychiatric social worker and follower of Freud, who frequently dispensed psychological advice. She was currently an expert on children because, though childless herself, she was head social worker at Belfaire, where those poor orphans lived. It was by eavesdropping on one of Aunt Celia's confidential conversations with Mom that I learned with horror that fingernail biting, my brother's vice, was an unconscious self-inflicted punishment for masturbation—a mortifying bit of theory that made me grateful to have overheard the news before I was tempted to bite my own. Another instance of our disparate fates, whereby Bob's humiliating secret was discovered, while mine was mercifully concealed behind long well-tended nails.

Mom continued: I asked the doctor why he thought this happened. In his opinion, you are going through a difficult phase of adolescent rebellion that will probably pass as you mature. I offered to take you to see him, but he said there was no need now, only if you showed further signs of being troubled.

Troubled? I did not feel troubled; I felt restive, constrained. Being the object of such earnest psychologizing made me long for air. It was almost as confining as Mom's taking upon herself all blame for my transgressions. What about me? Where did I fit in? What good was my remorse for what I'd done if Mom insisted my deviant acts were somehow really her fault? How could I claim my desires or profit from my mistakes if I were trapped in an inevitable *phase?* All their fancy explanations and hidden reasons obliterated my own motives and follies—my daring, my overweening confidence, my proud rebellion, even my blind stupidity, not least for having switched the price tags instead of just the sweaters, which I might have claimed as a mere mistake—and left no room for my need to test the boundaries of the bad as Bob struggled with the good. For it did not escape me that while my transgressions were experiments in willfulness, Bob's seemed more like inadvertent failures of control, drawing punishments he considered deeply unjust.

It had long been like that between us—beginning with our childish fights, which he usually started on the basis of his superior strength and size, but which I soon learned to win by slyly goading him to such rage that he lost control and pummeled me, for which he alone took the blame. Once during a fight he accidentally hit my head on the corner of the coffee table, drawing blood from me and punishment from Dad; after that for a brief time I was able to win our wrestling matches—probably because Bob was afraid of what might happen if he really let go, though at the time I believed it was due to my own quickness and strength during a lull in Bob's growth. How fearlessly I baited him then, before he took another sudden spurt that shot him way past me into a strapping youth I had no desire to wrestle. The punishments he received left him angry and morose, while mine kept me hopeful and plotting.

Now, for instance: with the storm of my dishonor dying down, the next item of business was to get my sentence reduced—or, short of that, to devise a way to sneak out a window. Because although I did not think three months' grounding an unfair punishment for a crime like mine, life was calling me.

*

Soon an entire outlaw realm outside my family's reach beckoned to me. In those postwar years, booming Cleveland sustained an underworld of after-hours spots and jazz dives, gambling casinos and racetracks, rumored drug rings and brothels, which struck me as more tantalizing and worldly than the dull familiar routines of Cleveland Heights High School with its undemanding classes and redundant social events. No wonder criminologists report the most crime-prone ages (albeit for boys) are fifteen to nineteen. Bored by the prudish, the feminine, the commonplace, I longed to burst out of that closed system where everything was predictable and known. With my boy's name and my good grades why shouldn't I sneak out of school to go to the races with the class tout, Dick Levinsky (whom I'd pulled through math), or the male-only pool hall on lunch hour, or the boys' department of May's, where I worked at Christmas, for accessories? Didn't Dad himself spurn conventional opinion? The forbidden and infamous now tempted me.

Not that I wanted ever again to tangle with the law. Stealing had been sheer folly, as rash and disappointing as the equally forbidden sexual intercourse, whose vaunted bliss eluded me in the rash moment when I succumbed to a boyfriend's entreaties. Still, I longed to escape that conventional world I saw closing in on me like fog and test myself against its mindless rules.

My underworld was like the movies. It inhabited just such nightclubs as the one portrayed in *Gilda*, which as a nubile adolescent I had watched a record number of eight times—and would have watched eight more had it not left our theater. "Put the blame on Mame, boys/Put the blame on Mame," vamped Rita Hayworth playing Gilda, a night-club performer, as she slowly stripped off one long glove and then the other, snapping them seductively at her audience. Her gown was practically falling off. I longed to be Mame—or Gilda. The Cleveland underworld, which, like *Gilda,* had crime as its premise, squired women nearly as sexy, who intrigued me nearly as much. That it was run by sleazy mobsters who maintained their hold by threat and force of death was as unreal to me as any movie.

For my voyeuristic purposes, entrée to this realm was easy. Not because of the sons and daughters (more accurately, nieces and nephews) of the underworld who were part of our high school crowd; one boy I briefly dated had lost his father to the mob, and a girl in my sorority, who was not particularly popular despite having more cashmere sweaters than anyone else, lived in a big Fairmont Boulevard mansion boasting a ballroom, a poolroom, and a wide Tara staircase, which we all knew had been purchased with dirty money. If anything, she and others I could mention tried to disclaim their shady connections. One classmate was so mortified when her uncle's name appeared in the newspaper that she stayed out of school. No, entrée was assured me because the gangsters and their molls were on exhibit every weekend at certain clubs—even the big numbers boss himself, the notorious Shondor Birns (Cleveland's "Public Enemy Number One" and owner of the best restaurant in town), whom if one was lucky one could sometimes glimpse downstairs at his private table at the glittering Alhambra Tavern talking on the phone, or late at night at the Theatrical Grill on Short Vincent Street, or at the Colony, or occasionally at the Café Tijuana, where I had seen Billie Holiday in person.

I say *glimpse* because like the sun, or the rock-sized diamond on his pinkie, Shondor Birns, with his natty clothes and big cigar, was thought to be too hot to look at directly. Rather, one schemed for a seat, preferably at a nearby table, that put him in one's direct line of vision so he would never know one was watching him. Then all one had to do was keep picking at one's steak or nursing one's drink and lighting up another cigarette, smiling at the dumb jokes of one's dumb date who hadn't known why one wanted to get dressed up and come to this joint in the first place. Like the movies. And if the seating didn't work out, one could watch instead the beautiful women who belonged to the gangsters. Like showgirls, they were openly on display— table-hopping, leaning over to get a light off some semi-stranger's gold Ronson cigarette lighter, pulling some reluctant young factotum or gangster-in-training onto the dance floor to do the rhumba, the samba, or the cha-cha-cha because their patrons were too busy conducting secret business to be bothered dancing. "Go on, doll, get Tommy-O to dance with you," one could occasionally overhear. I thought of them collectively as Shondor's girls, though each one had a man of her own, and I could have watched them forever with their extravagantly coiffed heads thrown back to expose their long swan throats, left palm on their midriff, hips gyrating, index finger in the air, and their perfect white teeth bared in a flashy smile as they twirled their silky dresses and kicked up their high-heeled shoes to the brassy music of the band. No question of jealousy here: the factotums returned the women promptly to their men, everyone knew who belonged to whom, even though one could see they were not the gangsters' wives, anyway not their original wives, they were far too gorgeous and lithe and tall and goddammit to be stuck in even the most elaborately equipped kitchen. They were my closest approach to movie stars, though it was rumored some of them might be call girls. The smartest of them got their men to buy them boutiques or half interests in beauty parlors like Portabello's, the busy salon in our suburb where my mother had her hair done every Thursday (for symphony), and I had mine done on occasional Fridays (for school dances), and every customer emerged with a signature Portabello look.

My mother and I had been going to Portabello's for years—Mom had a standing appointment with Aldo Portabello himself—before I realized that the stunning proprietors, Aldo and Gina Portabello, as well as some of the operators and customers, were regular Saturday nighters on the dance floor of the Alhambra Tavern. Then one Friday, when my appointed operator failed to show up, I was assigned to Karla, whom I recognized at once as one of Shondor's girls. I studied her closely in her pale green smock as she cut my hair and rolled it on rollers—the beautiful Karla with a whispery voice and delicately freckled transparent skin and long silky blond hair that contrasted so strikingly to the dark, willowy, long-necked, emaciated Portabellos. How different she was at work than when she was decked out and dancing! When I tried to draw her out, she, unlike other operators, had nothing to say. Was she shy? vacuous? aloof? cowed? I was disappointed to see how easily glamour could be tarnished, how quickly the forbidden became ordinary. When my upright parents joined their friends at Cleveland's outlawed Mounds Club for an evening of roulette, Mom in her black velvet off-the-shoulder gown, Dad awkward in a tux, the underworld began to lose its sheen.

"We went half a dozen times, won a few dollars, lost a few, it didn't interest us," said Dad as I pumped him long-distance for memories. "Why are you so curious about Shondor Birns anyway?"

Could he have forgotten? Hadn't my fascination played into his worst fears that I might sink into a life of crime, danger, sleaze, and sex? It lasted nearly a year, until the night I actually met Shondor. My racetrack buddy, Dick Levinsky, introduced us late one night at the Colony. No sooner did I look directly into Shondor's astigmatic eyes, get a whiff of his big cigar, and hear his undistinguished speech than my interest in him waned, soon to evaporate completely following another shake-up of the underworld, with its subsequent arrests and trials. Headlines screamed the news, with a picture of Shondor Birns himself, bare arms constrained by cops, glasses askew as he tried to hide his face from the camera. Gambling clubs and after-hours joints were raided. Brothels were shut down. The machine-gun nest cleverly concealed over the door of the Mounds Club was exposed along with a whole closetful of automatic guns and hundreds of rounds of ammo. With Shondor sentenced to the Warrensville Workhouse, many of the regulars at the Alhambra Tavern disappeared, and Shondor's girls, adrift in their drab daytime lives, searched for new men to take them dancing.

"But Daddy! You know I've always been interested in Shondor. You used to send me clippings about him whenever he was arrested. I still have them—that photo of him in jail in his underwear, and then on trial for the Mo Goldman slaying, with his beautiful young alibi sitting beside him. And the obituaries after he and his car were blown to smithereens. Don't you remember?"

"I believe it was your mother's idea. She thought that having met him once you'd be interested, though frankly, I never understood why."

Psychological complexity, particularly perversion or even mere recalcitrance, escaped the comprehension of a man like Dad, with simple upright opinions of the proper and right. That very week, on the phone he'd reported to me with agitation, "Your mother frustrates me."

"Why, Daddy?"

"She won't turn the wheel on her wheelchair."

"Why do you want her to turn it?"

"To go into the washroom."

"What does she say when you ask her to?"

"She says she can't."

"She probably can't, Daddy. You know she can't do anything on her own anymore without asking at every step, 'What should I do next?' "

"I don't see why she can't turn a little wheel!" he said. Two days later he again complained: "Your mother is very stubborn."

"Why?" I asked, ready, like a parent, to adjudicate.

"She wouldn't accompany me back to her room."

"Why not?"

"I don't know why not. She's stubborn. She just sat there, refusing to leave the dining room. A nurse had to take her back."

Still, he'd been right to dismiss my infatuation with Shondor's world. He must have sensed that my unarticulated yearnings were for a purposeful life, not just an offbeat one, though in our narrow hidebound circle I had no idea how to find one.

*

For my sixteenth birthday Mom bought me my own half-season seat for the Cleveland Orchestra, and I abandoned the cha-cha-cha. I was almost done with high school; Bob had started at Ohio State, where our cozy crowd, living in sorority and fraternity houses, were competing to nab the best catches to marry.

Frantic to escape that destiny, over the summer I'd begun to study the year's entire symphonic repertoire, like

Mom, playing my Beethoven, Brahms, and Stravinsky over and over on the phonograph. Like Dad, I delved into books for answers to the puzzles of life pressing in on me. Giving culture my own defiant twist, over my bed I hung an anonymous master's Pietà depicting a seminude Jesus stretched out on a pallet, which I found ravishingly sexy. Starting in the fall, every other Thursday night, seated in the orchestra between my parents, like my mother I let the music whip up my surging desires. But like my father I struggled to control them.

Only two lives seemed open to me: theirs. If I followed my friends down the easy road to Ohio State, then no matter how I might cultivate the "finer things" Mom promoted, I would be destined to repeat her limited life of marriage, motherhood, housewifery. It would be irrevocably settled the moment I registered for my first class. My only other choice was to follow Dad and become a lawyer. By 1950, when I graduated from high school, law was a male profession all but closed to women, but Mom's oldest sister, Lilian, had set a family precedent by taking a law degree in 1922. Though she never practiced, becoming instead a court stenographer, and scandalized the Davis family by running off to Chicago with a married man and eventually marrying another man half her age ("What do you know about Lil's activities?" Dad wrote to Mom early in their marriage. "I've always said there's something strange and secret about her conduct and your family's relations with her"), there was her striking Davis profile in cap and gown in the top row of the Cleveland Law School class picture, one of ten women among a hundred men, proving that law had not always been an impossible hope for an ambitious girl.

I was still under my mother's spell, inhaling like perfume her easy laugh, her flair, the earnest incline of her head as she asserted her opinions, the seductive force with which she pressed her causes (including mine). But somehow, at the last minute, remembering my birthright, I resisted the lure of Ohio State.

Of course Dad was tickled, if surprised, to see his dormant influence coming up to the finish line—especially since Bob had no interest in the law. He encouraged me to apply to Western Reserve, a private university of incontestable seriousness right there in Cleveland, which had served my mother, aunts, and uncles well enough, and would have served Dad too, he said, had he been able to afford college. Tuition was higher than at public colleges like Ohio State, but the savings incurred by living at home would equalize the cost and even help pay for law school. He typed my application, as he typed my term papers if a deadline was near, like no other dad I knew, letting his fingers fly over the keys while I at his elbow read aloud my illegible drafts, dense like his with interlinear refinements.

I was exhilarated by my last-minute reprieve. It meant I would not have to leave them yet, would not yet have to choose. It was the same relief I now experienced, forty-five years later, every time I heard Dad's frail but cheerful voice reassure me long-distance that the miracle was holding, they were still all right, and I did not yet have to relinquish them to mortality.

Chapter 9

Now I wonder why I'd once felt such urgency to choose between my parents, as if I were doomed to repeat the devastating choice forced upon me by the department store manager. Was the conflict between them deeper than I knew, deep enough to possess me? Or was my struggle really about my birthright, that rare gift to a girl of a father's blessing—so rare that I spent much of my adolescent energy trying to break the bonds of convention and lay claim to it. It was the source of what Mom termed my "difficult adolescence," my friends called my kookiness, and today is known simply as gender trouble.

With my boy's name and my birthright, I had to strike out on my own. That was the meaning of the road, the frontier, the territory, dreamed of by every ambitious boy. It was the American imperative, the purpose for which generations of immigrants had with stoic sacrifice set their sons free. It was the sine qua non of every mythic hero who, to win a place in the world, must abruptly cut his ties and slay a monster. Both my grandfathers had left their parents in Eastern Europe never to see them again. But how was I, a girl, still deeply attached to my parents and living comfortably at home, to cut loose?

I found my ways. No sooner did I register for classes at Western Reserve University than I got myself a boyfriend with a beard. In 1950s Cleveland, nothing could be more unusual. Max Kaplan's was the only beard any of us had ever seen in Cleveland, aside from the few worn by the religious or Orthodox, whom Dad called fanatics. Since growing my own beard was out of the question despite my name and birthright, when I saw Max's in the library, I quickly nabbed it for myself.

A graduate student in English literature who hobnobbed with professors, Max had recently immigrated with his parents to Cleveland from England. As a poor scholarship boy, he had taken a Cambridge degree under the famous literary scholar F. R. Leavis. Along with the beard, Max's erudition, underscored by his English accent, dazzled me. Not counting my grandparents, he was my first contact with a foreign culture and also my first intellectual. Until college, I didn't know a single person in Cleveland outside my family who voluntarily read books. Although my brother constantly teased me about the beard and mimicked the accent, I was glad to reap the benefit of Max's Cambridge education.

Before I met Max, my goal had been to get my degree quickly and go straight to law school, following Dad's speedy footsteps right past the secretaries into his inner office. This goal, novel for a girl, justified the otherwise suspect arrangement of my living at home. Until foolish Max challenged me.

Pedantic, smug, and insecure, Max used his English superiority against us. While riding around in my parents' car, he patronized Bob's philistinism, Dad's prudery, and above all, what he called Mom's bourgeois pretentions. Affecting a sophisticated manner that merged F. R. Leavis (the raised finger, the subtlety) and D. H. Lawrence (the beard, the rant), Max elevated himself by condescending to us, reserving his slyest slurs for my mother.

Why did he do it? Perhaps he considered his cosmopolitan critique of our provincial world a crucial part of my education, or maybe he envied my privileged life. Most likely he was simply expressing the era's contempt for American mothers popularized by Philip Wylie in his best-selling 1942 essay collection, *Generation of Vipers,* with its infamous matriphobic diatribe against "Momism," both reflecting and unleashing a virulent misogyny.

Before Max's (and Wylie's) attack I'd been proud of my parents. Now my pride, once as comforting as cream, began to curdle into shame. Max's relentless snickers and innuendos struck me where I lived in reasonable harmony with my family. There I was in college, enjoying all the comforts of home, commuting to class in the family car while Dad rode the bus to work, blasting my music through the living room at any hour, borrowing my mother's clothes, monopolizing their telephone, accompanying them to symphony every other Thursday, relishing having them to myself with Bob off at Ohio State, when Max began to enlighten me.

Of course, what hit them hit me. To defend them was to condemn myself. Not to defend them was to betray them.

I remember the scene but not the words of my betrayal. Max and I were alone in the Ashurst kitchen snacking on chili Mom had left for us—a thoughtful act Max chose to disparage. When I tried to defend her, he turned his aspersions on me. Though he too lived with his parents, he challenged the ease of my living with mine, insinuating uncritical attachments, oedipal longings, bourgeois benefits. Horrified to be thus nailed, I was shamed into submission. Scrambling to defend myself, I tried to dump all my bourgeois guilt into my mother's lap where it wouldn't hurt me.

Long accustomed to my lapses, she may not even have noticed. Not so Dad. You know, Al, he chided me, I fear you sometimes don't appreciate just how unusual a woman your mother is. He was right. In my frenzy to distance myself I disavowed the very notion of family bonds: parents were mere temporary provisional caretakers with no special claims. Invoking reason's superiority to irrational sentiment, I contended that my chance descent from a random combination of egg and sperm lodged fortuitously in a certain womb gave my parents no more claim to me than they had to my adopted brother: parenthood was nothing but an arbitrary legal arrangement.

Such a display of weakness and hypocrisy could not go unpunished. Like Dad, I believed in justice—but with a difference: to him it was a benign force governing the world, while to me it was an invisible threat that would one day make me pay. For what? For the unnamed crimes of taking love for granted and (in Bob's words) getting away with murder. If justice knew the fairy tales, it would make my children commit those very crimes on me. Hoping to escape punishment, I prudently vowed to have no children. In the meantime, barely a sophomore, I disclaimed responsibility for my betrayal, blaming Max instead. Stung by his criticism, resentful that he had divided me against myself and forced my treachery, I soon fell in love with a genuine professor—married and twice my age—and made Max my "beard": perfect cover for my secret affair. And when Max transferred to the Yale Graduate School on a full scholarship bestowed by a wealthy benefactor I found for him, I savored the irony of his eager acceptance of my bourgeois bounty.

*

That affair with my professor, my first great passion—how can I do it justice in this age which, in its zeal to protect young women from sexual predators, sometimes fails to distinguish between welcome and unwelcome sex?

Once I became a serious student, my professors invaded my imagination, and some my body too. The first was an unpleasant fellow with a head of wavy auburn hair like Dad's who, I am ashamed to say, gave me my first orgasm, which horrified me with its appalling tingling of fingers and toes that refused to stop as I lay gasping on a table in the science lab. The second was a young psychology instructor who kept me after class for "therapy," which meant sessions of sex talk in his office that culminated one Saturday morning in a private conference in a nearby motel room. I shudder to remember both of those compromising episodes. Finally there was my first great love—of mind, body, and soul—on whom I set my sights at eighteen, then loved actively every day until I graduated college at twenty. He was my mentor and inspiration. For the knowledge and passion, the confidence and ambition he instilled in me, I continue to honor him, despite his weaknesses and crimes.

He was a huge, almost ugly, ungainly man with a lecherous leer that pierced right through his glasses, and a deep nasal voice that lowered nearly to a whisper as he lay one finger alongside his fleshy nose and leaned forward, eyes gleaming, to issue some outrageous intellectual challenge. He had lost the sight of one eye, but not the wicked gleam. He had, I believe, only one suit, grey, baggy, and shiny, and one frayed tweed overcoat—not a bourgeois thread to his name. Through relentless questioning he led his students down an unknown path into a dark cave where incongruities and contradictions assaulted you; then when your mind's eyes had adjusted to the dark, he would tease you back to the light. His provocative questions, for which he refused to supply answers, were perfectly aimed to expose your biases and force you to rethink your hidden assumptions. His controversial insinuations kept his students huddled around him after every class and trailing him all over campus.

Of course my parents knew nothing of my affair—nothing, that is, of the sex—until the end. But I could hardly disguise my infatuation. It burst from all my conversations in *Campbell this* and *Campbell that.* His initials covered my notebooks. I took every course he offered and parroted his teachings, elevating my ambition from law to philosophy. Though I tried to keep order in the various compartments of my life, strictly forbidding Campbell to phone me at home, in my secret heart I knew that my burgeoning sexual feelings had everything to do with my parents. Instead of loosening my family ties, the force and secrecy of my affair only twisted them more tightly.

Before long I developed a craving to have my mother and Campbell meet. I thought they would see in each other what I saw in them—they were the same age, both devoted themselves to worthy causes and international policy, both overflowed with curiosity and vitality. I hoped that if she met him even once she would share my enthusiasm and maybe bestow her blessing; I felt that unless he experienced for himself her original, exuberant charms he would never fully understand me. Perhaps I wanted to vie with her for him and win. Whatever my game, it was too dangerous to involve Dad; I wanted no part of those two men eyeing each other suspiciously or, worse, squaring off.

My Aunt Celia lived near campus in a tiny two-room apartment overflowing with books and music. Now that my life too centered on books and music, I began to visit her sometimes at the end of a day, before Uncle Leon got home from his work as a shoe salesman ready to practice his violin. As dusk descended, we sat in her magic space drinking coffee from tiny cups in deep discussion of music, ideas, politics, and art. Sometimes she pressed sophisticated new books on me: Kafka's diaries, the Berlin stories of Christopher Isherwood, avant-garde novels by the young Paul Bowles and Truman Capote. Sometimes she carefully lowered the diamond-tipped needle over her turntable and, with her nostrils flared and an expectant smile at the corners of her Davis lips, played me a precious new recording: a Bach violin sonata, perhaps, or Beethoven's *Archduke Trio,* or a concerto by Bartók or Shostakovich. I thought her the one person in the world who might begin to understand the confused turmoil of my feelings, my complicated predicament. Not that I dared tell her about my illicit affair with Campbell, but I hoped that, trained as she was, she might read beneath my earnest questions. I was relieved when one day she suggested that I might want to see a psychiatrist. She knew just the man and promised to smooth the way with my parents, no questions asked.

About that time, my unconscious had begun to wonder if my mother might not also be in a liaison with a married man. I didn't articulate the question even to myself; I was too far over my head in my own tumultuous affair to be able to consider or even acknowledge hers. To the psychiatrist, Dr. Gerhardt Stern, the closest I ever came was to say that I thought my father loved my mother more than she loved him—which, though I certainly felt for Dad, seemed the right model for me to follow should I ever marry. (The mood is confirmed by one of my freshman themes I found in a folder in a box in the Shaker attic. Entitled "The Great Illusion," it begins: "Thesis: Because of our modern American way of life, mate selection must result from intelligent analysis, rather than from romantic love, if successful marriages are to ensue.") Sidestepping the doctor's oedipal theories, I insisted that if he were to understand me at all he should look to my Cleveland Heights cohort, not my family. (Long before feminism I was already a social constructionist.) When he clung to his hypotheses, I presumed that a doctor transplanted from Vienna to Cleveland was incapable of understanding the suffocating social stranglehold of suburban Ohio that had siphoned my best energies into endless sniping efforts to resist. Cleveland! I railed—and might have added, the 1950s! could I have imagined an alternate future.

I was fond of Mom's friend Kenneth, sometimes secretly fancied him for myself. He was a cultivated man with big moist soulful eyes, expressive nostrils, a high forehead, and thinning hair who never came to visit empty-handed. He lived in a large Shaker house and ran the sort of business (I don't know what) that enabled him to spend a lot of time outside his office. For years, beginning at least as far back as my last year in high school, he was often, then always, at our house. He and my mother were together every afternoon, and in the evenings when it wasn't the two of them it was the four of them—Mom and Dad and Kenneth and his wife, Anne—going to Kenneth and Anne's country club or to a party or concert. Sometimes Anne, a brittle blond woman with a slight lisp whom I didn't like, took Mom "antiquing" with her, a hobby Mom thought too rich for herself, and Dad feared. In retrospect, I can smell the sex hanging in the air, though at the time I believed they were all four just good friends.

It must surely have been those sexual vibes between Mom and Kenneth that made me want her to meet Campbell. After weeks of anticipation I managed to pull it off. I invited Mom to meet me in a campus snack bar, where

Campbell just happened to be having coffee. Oh, look! There's Professor Campbell. Would you like to meet him? I said. I waved him over to our table, and then the three of us sat together sipping coffee and talking, they in their forties, I in my teens. As I watched my titans circle one another and draw each other out, I felt as if I were tying an extravagant bow of the dangling ribbons of my life.

Well, what did you think? I asked each of them afterward. Mom said she liked my professor very much. She said she was glad to have finally met him and hoped to see him again, which excited me. But Campbell's response was melancholy, as if he had seen in my love for my elegant mother our approaching end.

He was right, of course. We had not spoken of permanence, and as the time neared for me to leave for graduate school, I knew I must make the break. My life lay ahead; philosophy and New York beckoned. (Philosophy—awakened in me by his contagious passion for ideas. New York—where one Christmas vacation he and I had spent four sizzling days alone together in the luxury of a hotel bedroom, with time out only for him to put in a brief appearance at his academic conference and for us to grab an occasional bite to eat.) When we were discovered at one of our trysting places by his wife—a wife and mother, I saw with horror, like my own mother—I knew the affair was over. But when I tried to break it off, he grew agitated and refused. This is not something you can decide unilaterally, he said gravely. We met several more times, each one ending in frustration and argument.

Then it was finals week of my final semester as an undergraduate. I needed to settle matters quickly so I could study for exams, which was already difficult because the inside of our house was being painted, and everything was in disarray. With my parents temporarily sleeping downstairs and my room covered with drop cloths, my bed, which had been moved into the upstairs hall, seemed the only place where I could study. The disruption reminded me of the terrible night Aunt Jeannette had died, and by the end of that weekend I had bitten off all my fingernails.

I was up late studying in bed, papers spread around me, when the phone rang. I knew enough to dash for it. It was Campbell, saying he had to see me. Reluctantly I drove to one of our street-corner rendezvous, and at his insistence I got into his car to talk. Over my veto he drove us to a secluded spot where he tried to make love to me. I pulled away. I needed to get back home and study. But he ignored my objections and forced himself on me. I was furious; I thought of biting off his penis. But in the end I submitted, resolving not to see him again.

Two days later I was on the top floor of the college library, a favorite study place because it was almost always empty. Campbell came charging up the stairs two at a time. I need to talk to you right away, he said, yanking my hand. I pulled back, refusing to go with him, insisting I had to study. Then—I don't know how it happened exactly—he was dragging me toward the stairs, toward the one spot of the curved banister that plunged straight past the three tall flights to the ground floor. I believed—I was certain!—he intended to throw me over the banister down that stairwell.

Somehow I pulled myself free and tore down the stairs, leaving him behind. Then in terror for my life, after years of secrecy, swallowing my pride, I went straight to my father and confessed. A brief lawyer letter—citing a statute and my age and ending, "if you attempt to contact my daughter again I shall press charges"—set me free.

The embarrassment I endured in revealing my sexual

passion to my prudish father was small compared to the shame I felt at asking him to rescue me. How humiliating to need a parent's help in my grown-up game, particularly after the heady illusion of independence conferred by my long, clandestine affair.

This time as he bailed out his errant daughter my father did not cry.

*

Even in his nineties, with his powers greatly diminished, Dad remained the rescuer. Many months after Mom had made what her nurses in the dementia ward called a "reasonable adjustment" to her new surroundings, she suddenly began to balk. She grew angry over any disruption of routine—a mandatory bath, a beauty parlor visit, a nurse's overstrenuous urging that she take her pills at bedtime. One night, after I'd returned from Judson to the Shaker house, in a rage she demanded that her husband be called at once. When Dad was on the phone, she said, "Take me home, Sam, come take me home."

Dad calmed her down by promising to see her in the morning. But by the time he arrived the next day, she'd forgotten all about her feelings of the night before, believing, he reported to me at lunch, that the whole episode—her fury, the phone call, Dad's promise to return—had all been part of a dream.

"What did you dream, Mom?" I asked her.

"It was awful," she said. "I dreamed that Sam was angry with me because we were out of synch—I was living in the 1940s, and he was living now." (How astute was her unconscious!) "I called him up and begged him, please don't be angry with me, Bummer. And he said, 'Don't you worry, Bummer, I'm not angry.' But I knew he was."

A few days later, after I'd gone back to Maine, Dad reported to me that Mom had again grown agitated, refused to take her pills, and complained that she was being held prisoner. "Sam," she said when the nurse again got him on the phone, "they're keeping me here against my will. Take me home, Sammy. Please. I want to come home."

It was more than he could bear. The next day he commandeered a wheelchair and kidnapped his wife of sixty-five years. He helped her into the chair, piled nightgown, slippers, and toothbrush on her lap, then, huffing and puffing, wheeled her past the double doors of Breuning to the elevator, up a ramp, and on through the halls to his apartment. After putting her to bed, he returned to her room for her clothes and her indispensable medicines.

I was thrilled by the news. My frail but indomitable father, as dependable as always, had once again rushed to the rescue. Now they were back together. Once more I could speak to Mom every day as I used to do. I rejoiced in her pleasure and relief, though I knew they couldn't last.

Within days Dad reported that she was refusing to take her medications.

"Mom," I said when he handed her the phone, "Dad says you're giving him a hard time about taking your medicine. Is it true?"

"Oh, no!" she answered. "Sam and I never quarrel. Never! Of course I take my medicine. It's nothing. One tiny pill in the morning, one at night." Then: "Oh, it's so good to be home! Everything looks so beautiful. I know all this furniture so well, except one small chest."

She was right; everything in that apartment, except a small chest that came from Dad's office, she had selected to furnish their Shaker house.

"Oh, if you could see how lovely it looks here," she said,

her voice pleading. "That picture—what is it?—the Kent Rockwell. It looks as if it were made for this place."

What matter that she'd reversed the artist's names? She was happy. Indeed, it was almost like old times, as Dad prepared their breakfasts and lunches in his small kitchen and chivalrously gave Mom his walker to go to Fisher Dining Room, where he ordered dinner for two.

Soon all Judson was in an uproar—meetings, consultations, evaluations. Strenuously I took my parents' side, though Dr. Murphy was skeptical. "This will be too much for Sam," he warned me, and I feared that without his approval the arrangement couldn't last. But no matter what anyone said, Dad refused to let Mom go.

When the staff called a special conference to deal with the problem, I flew to Judson from Maine. It was late summer; outside Fisher Dining Room the geraniums and begonias were still in riotous bloom, and beyond the windows of Dad's apartment a blanket of flowering shrubs, dotted by pockets of flowers and lush ornamental trees, stretched up the long landscaped hillside. An interior person in every sense, Dad barely noticed as he sat reading in his favorite chair beneath the slow turning of the ceiling fan. But Mom, a visual sybarite, was filled with joy at the sight. I shared her joy, not for summer but for her happiness, however fleeting.

The staff decided to wait and see—until Dr. Murphy examined my father two weeks later and pronounced him too weak to care for Mom. After many long-distance skirmishes with the administration, we reached a provisional compromise: Mom could spend every other day at Dad's apartment from midmorning on, after she'd had her meds, and nights back in her room on the fifth floor of Breuning, to which an aide would wheel her after she dined with Dad in Fisher.

"How's the new arrangement working out?" I asked Mom after a week. "Is it okay sleeping in Breuning?"

"Of course," she said. "Breuning is like a second home to me. It's very familiar."

Not, however, familiar enough to prevent her getting lost as she bumped her walker to her room. Every step or two she asked, perplexed, "Now where should I go?" It was a short walk from the fifth-floor lunchroom, but not till she got to the D wing, marked by a large letter *D* on the wall, did she know where she was. "*D* is for Dorothy!" she proclaimed with delight and turned right, to her room.

"It should be familiar, Mom. You sleep there."

"Sometimes, I guess."

"Every night."

"I do?" she asked. "Are you sure?"

"Yes, Mom, quite sure." But so, I reminded her, had she and Dad slept in separate bedrooms in their Shaker house.

"We did?" she asked, incredulous.

This question signaled a subtle change for the worse. Until then it had been mainly short-term memories that had deserted her. But the separate bedrooms she and Dad had maintained for forty years were housed in long-term memory. Unlike her cancer or my abandonment, which she might well have wanted to forget, the achievement of a room of her own had been one of her constant satisfactions. Now, evidently, long-term pleasures too had begun to go.

iii A Simple Movement

This most simple of movements, the turning of your back . . .

— JAMAICA KINCAID, *The Autobiography of My Mother*

Mom and Dad at the Temple of
Apollo. Delphi, Greece, 1961

Chapter 10

Once, after twenty years of living away, I returned to the Heights for a book signing to which all my high school friends were invited. That was in the early 1970s, when the country was in the throes of tremendous cultural upheaval. The smoldering social movements of the 1960s had burst into flame, we were at war in Vietnam, and I had become a passionate feminist, activist, and writer. Yet so little seemed to have changed in our suburb that I felt as if I were in a time warp.

Returning again two decades later, this time for a class reunion, I was amazed anew by how little had changed. More of our crowd than I'd ever have guessed were still married to their high school sweethearts or the catches they famously landed in college before dropping out. Dick Levinsky was still a racetrack bum, Stan Grilli still grabbed the mike and sang, half the basketball team worked as managers or salesmen for their old buddy, real estate mogul Herm Herman, cracking the same cynical sexist jokes. They danced the way we used to dance, the women cast critical eyes on one another's clothes, they met for lunch in the same old groups, were scandalized by the same stories. ("Why would you ever want to leave?" asked my friend Susan.)

It was true that by then everything that could happen

to them had happened, just like elsewhere. They'd married, reproduced, traveled, divorced, remarried, started businesses, made a bundle, gone bust, got elected to the board, resigned in disgrace, hit the bottle, kicked it, lost it all in Vegas, had passionate affairs, got caught in flagrante delicto, taken bribes, done coke, had facelifts, made a comeback, lost weight, gotten fat. They'd suffered with their addicted children and autistic grandchildren. They'd buried their mothers and survived their fathers-in-law. They'd endured disappointment, indifference, ingratitude, mastectomies, hysterectomies, aneurysms, bypasses, transplants, implants, and every kind of cancer known to medicine. Yet their lives seemed essentially the same. Even those who flew in from retirement condos in distant states might as well never have left (though Fran did take me aside to ask searchingly, "Tell me, how did you ever find the nerve to leave?").

I thought I'd never willingly return to Cleveland, never be comfortable there again. The Heights felt unreal to me, not life but a parody of life. Yet since I'd taken charge of my parents' affairs, I felt it gradually regain reality. Arriving at the house from the airport began to feel as ordinary as returning home from work. My past and present were moving closer; if anything, it was my other life that sometimes seemed unreal.

Shortly after five I left the house to wait for the realtor. Sitting on the stone steps, looking past the long front lawn with its flutter of fallen leaves, I watched the black housekeepers, done with their work, gather with their shopping bags across Shaker Boulevard to wait for the downtown Rapid to carry them home. Otherwise, not a human in sight except the occasional white man in topcoat and leather gloves, sporting regulation briefcase and newspaper, who descended the steps of an arriving train to disappear up a street. Same class divisions as always, as everywhere.

Yet in the last decade Shaker Heights, I'd been told, had become a model of middle-class racial integration, as you could see in all the restaurants and shops on Shaker Square. Things were changing even on the Heights, and of course there was much more to Cleveland than the Heights. For the first time I wondered how I might have lived, what I might have done, had I chosen to stay.

Promptly at five-thirty the realtor, whom I'd known since junior high, pulled into the driveway. We were to confer about the interior now that repairs were completed and the house was scheduled for reinspection. When I offered tea, she declined. Clearly her life—busy, efficient, "professional," as she would say—was no parody.

After pausing in each room for a critical look, she outlined my tasks: rearrange furniture, store pictures, take up carpeting, have the Electric Chair removed, hide the knick-knacks, and in every way negate my parents' presence in the house. "We want to strike the right combination of lived-in and empty. Because frankly," she said, "buyers would rather not have to imagine the former owners. They want to visualize themselves living here."

Yes! I thought when the realtor left and I went to work: just so had I in my youth tried to negate my parents' presence in my life in order to visualize myself.

*

"This most simple of movements, the turning of your back, is among the most difficult to make, but once it has been made you cannot imagine it was at all hard to accomplish," writes Jamaica Kincaid, as the heroine of *The Autobiog-*

raphy of My Mother cuts loose from her family. Delia Ephron, in her novel *Hanging Up,* describes the very moment: " 'Bye, Dad. Bye, Mom. I'll miss you.' Big lie. I got in line and didn't look back." These writers had their reasons, as does each of us; every story is unlike every other; and one must leave even the most agreeable family. Auden, who put an ocean between himself and his family, wrote: "An agreeable family life [is] a threat to . . . artistic and intellectual life. If the atmosphere were not so charming, it would be less of a temptation." The unremarkable progression: you're born, you grow up, you turn your back. And if you're lucky, you turn back again.

I moved to New York at twenty and broke the family spell. That was it. They were there; I was here. With a great tear, I moved, married, and ripped the cloth. My conflict was over. No longer would I have to choose which of them to follow.

To have my life I had to leave them. I couldn't split my heart in two—half his, half hers; half here, half there; each half anguishing over the other half. To protect them from knowledge of me that might make them suffer, I had to make them suffer. Cold turkey or no turkey. To escape the vise of their struggles, I had to cut myself free of their opinions. Then, having wrenched myself away, how endlessly, hopelessly, I asserted my difference—until my past was obliterated. How deeply it mattered! Home—that place that had once been so exquisitely particular to me as to seem incompatible with each adjacent suburb—became a mere speck on that flat undifferentiated mass New Yorkers dismiss as "Midwest." Ohio, Iowa, Omaha—the very names were alike, with their repetitive open vowels, flat and predictable as the geography, lacking the suspense of hard consonants. New York, "the city most expert and ruthless in destroying its past," as Alfred Kazin wrote, where loneliness is failure and memory indulgence, became my home. Systematically I toughened my vocabulary, thickened my dentals, purged my wardrobe as, with Mom's ambition and Dad's diligence, I turned my back.

Surrounded in New York by students, bohemians, and leftists, before a year was up I announced my intention to marry a graduate student my parents had never met (I barely knew him myself) and lead the life of the mind. This was a far cry from the relentless marriage code of Cleveland Heights, which decreed the best provider the best husband. Or was it? In 1953, when old maids started forming at twenty, and all want ads were headed "Help Wanted, Male," for jobs with a future, and "Help Wanted, Female," for dead-end jobs, the simplest way for a middle-class midwestern woman to follow a certain path was to marry it. If a shortage of funds was the price of my new life, I had but to renounce my desire for things. This I did easily, exultantly, as if it were my own superior idea, ignoring that Dad had shown me the frugal road and that Mom had convinced him to finance a year of graduate school. We flew to Cleveland for our wedding and back to New York for our honeymoon. Then gradually my contact with my parents dwindled to the duty phone call, the occasional letter, the annual visit, the rare dramatic rescue.

Mom scrambled to adapt: I was her married daughter working in New York City, she would say, giving the words a glamorous spin as they danced off her tongue. My daughter does social research, she works for a large bank, she does educational testing, she's an advertising librarian, she's an editor of an encyclopedia—and her husband is a professor at Columbia!

Anyway, they had Bob, didn't they? Bob, who with me gone finally had them to himself.

Just as I moved with my new husband into a one-room basement studio on Amsterdam Avenue in proud rejection of my bourgeois past, Mom found her Shaker dream house. For years she'd been house hunting in Shaker Heights with Kenneth or Anne, occasionally with Aunt Celia. Not seriously, since Dad strenuously opposed the project, but hungrily. Then she found it—a white elephant that cost not much more than they could get for the Ashurst house and offered more than twice the space. A gracious English-style brick colonial, it had mahogany paneling in the formal dining room and library, a servant's suite for Grandma Davis should Grandpa die, three elm trees to shade the front lawn, a back garden, and a Rapid stop right across the street.

How could Dad resist her arguments and entreaties? The house was clearly a sound investment, a steal, he had to agree—though what they would do with so much space now that the children were gone he couldn't begin to imagine.

Just leave that to me, said Mom. *I* know what to do with it.

He thought of the fix-up costs and the cost of furnishing all those rooms, but she promised to accept any budget he proposed. She would furnish it slowly, secondhand, using the skills she'd learned antiquing with Anne. As with everything that caught her interest, she was prepared to read and study and digest until she was expert, then form her own opinions. She would invest cautiously, wisely. And she wanted the house so badly.

From my savvy mother I learned that if you have a devoted mate, then a lover, however absorbing, is dispensable.

Her love affair with Kenneth was limited, discreet, and familiar, whereas a house—and such a house!—was open-ended, multifarious, and new, rendering it potentially even more absorbing. A house can be a large bare canvas on which to create yourself anew, using every color in your palette—your ambitions, hopes, talents, tastes, imagination—not unlike the beginnings of a love affair. Into the picture can be painted everything you hold dear. Everything except one thing—because nothing comes without a price. As Mom confessed to me years later, Dad set the price. *Okay, Bummer,* he said after she'd finally worn him down, *I'll move if that will bring you back to me.*

They were there, I was here. Their new life was a blank to me, as mine, I trusted, was to them. I heard that not long after they moved to Shaker Boulevard, Kenneth died of a stroke, and some years later Anne, his widow, followed. Several years after I left, Bob married a girl from Columbus, a pretty, dark-eyed schoolteacher, as Mom had been. They had the big white wedding that I, partly to spare Dad the expense, had foregone for myself. I flew in for it—see?—there we are, Bob beaming over his bride, the men in white dinner jackets, we in our pale-green organza dresses flared over our crinolines, with matching satin pumps and tiny veiled hats, smiling like movie stars among the out-of-towners. One picture of all the Kateses, one of all the Davises, with Johnny and Bob and me in both. The grandmas have new dresses. Their corsages are gardenias. And both grandfathers are dead.

*

The next time Dad rescued me, I didn't ask him to. Indeed, having grown up in that secretive family, I would have done anything I could to keep my parents ignorant of my sexual escapades—which was half the reason I, like so many, had left home. But my husband had other ideas.

Having dropped out of grad school to help support us, I was a twenty-three-year-old receptionist bored by my marriage when my husband applied for a Fulbright to study in Germany. I had married him for his gentleness, conversation, the life of the mind, but all I got was the gentleness: it turned out that he studied and wrote but he didn't much talk. I dared to hope that a stimulating year abroad might enliven our marriage.

In 1955 going abroad was a tremendous undertaking for a young person from Cleveland, involving a week on the open seas just to launch it. For my contribution to the enterprise, I skimped and saved every penny I could out of my minimal clerical salary by adopting three simple rules that outdid even Dad: postpone each purchase as long as possible, never buy a new one if the old one will do, and choose the cheapest.

When my husband won the fellowship, I was jubilant. Mom came to New York to see us off. She took me shopping for new clothes and announced that she and Dad planned to supplement my husband's modest stipend to enable us to travel a bit in Europe. As they had not yet been abroad themselves, and our financial separation had taken effect the moment I married, I was moved by their generous offer. Indeed, being with Mom again that week felt like old times, as we shopped, giggled, and wove fantasies together.

From the top deck of the student ship my husband and I waved our handkerchiefs down at her, gaily waving back. Yet as I left my mother behind again, this time across an ocean and a year, I felt beneath my smile the same grimace of pain she futilely tried to conceal behind her own unconvincing grin.

....

An adventurous interlude is no more likely to revive a fading marriage than moving house or having babies. Restless in Germany, over Christmas I took off for Spain. I urged my husband to come along, but he declined, preferring to spend the month on his research—which was fine with me.

Before I married, with rationalist enthusiasm I had championed what was then called "free love." To accommodate my husband, who resisted my views, upon marriage I abandoned the practice but not the principle. Once again on my own, if only for a month, I reasserted my hard-won prerogative.

No sooner did I cross the border than I found exactly what I'd been hungering for: a young Spanish actor who strummed a guitar and looked like Jean-Paul Belmondo. Part of a traveling troupe that performed classical drama at one-night stands in villages all over Spain, Luis invited me to share his bed. Suddenly sprung from three years of confining marriage, I fancied myself a Hemingway heroine. When my month was up and I returned to Germany, I was so in thrall to my fantasy that I found the nerve to leave my husband. Once having decided, I couldn't wait, not with all of Europe beckoning. Besides, I had missed my period, and fearing I might be pregnant by my Spanish lover, I needed to act quickly.

My husband was beside himself. A Spanish lover! He thought I'd gone mad. Since nothing he could say would dissuade me from leaving immediately, he resorted to extreme measures. Behind my back he cabled my parents that I had completely lost my mind and got myself pregnant by an unknown Spanish actor. Even though he, my husband, was ready to forgive me, in my crazed state I had abandoned all reason and, if nothing was done to stop me, was about to leave for parts unknown in pursuit of a dangerous abortion.

Imagine my parents' response to this news, given our family history of obstetric tragedy. I knew nothing of my husband's cable until a portly German gentleman suddenly appeared at the door of our small underheated apartment on the outskirts of town just as I was packing to leave.

Frau ———? he said, removing his hat as I opened the door.

Ja?

He stomped the snow from his galoshes, removed his gloves, and with a slight bow presented his card. Herr Doktor Hoffman, he said in assertive yet kindly tones. His bushy eyebrows and greying temples lent an air of authority to a face made jolly by red cheeks, red lips.

I looked around me. The room was a mess. Packing boxes and suitcases covered the floor; piles of clothing, books, papers, souvenirs were spread over every surface.

My husband has gone out, I said, but you are welcome to wait for him here. I examined the card. The word *Psychiater* followed Dr. Hoffman's name.

I thought it completely unlike my husband to seek sudden psychiatric help, despite his current state of agitation. I wondered if it was perhaps a play for my sympathy, designed to keep me from leaving. If so, why not tell the doctor my side?

Ein moment, I said. Please excuse the mess. I cleared off a place on the sofa and invited him to sit.

As soon as he was seated, Dr. Hoffman conveyed that he had come to see not my husband but me.

I was astounded. Me? Why me? Who had sent him?

That was simple, explained the doctor. A colleague in Vienna had telephoned him on behalf of a certain Dr. Gerhardt Stern of Cleveland, Ohio, USA (my old psychiatrist!), from whom he had received an urgent cable requesting an emergency consultation on my mental state (my *Geisteszustand*).

Seeing my husband behind this, I was incensed. In his rage at me he had involved my innocent parents in our private marital dispute. After such a cowardly and despicable act no wonder he'd suddenly disappeared! What sympathy I'd felt for his plight now dissolved in fury. However he felt about me, he had no right to drag in my poor parents who, as he well knew, were powerless to influence me. All that his bungling had accomplished was needless anxiety and suffering—and now this awkward visit.

Despite the language barrier—Dr. Hoffman's halting English was no better than my futile German—I saw my task clearly. The packing would have to wait. Handing the hefty German-English dictionary to Herr Doktor and keeping the English-German for myself, I cleared off another place on the sofa, sat down beside him, and prepared to establish if I could not only my sanity but the soundness of my decision to leave.

When my husband returned an hour later, we were deep in translation on the sofa. The doctor rose as I made the introductions. My husband seemed surprised, confused, and not a little embarrassed by the presence of a doctor summoned by my parents across an ocean. After they exchanged some words in German, Dr. Hoffman bowed to me and shook my hand. Then he put on his galoshes, hat, and gloves and left with my husband—no doubt to hear his side—and I proceeded with my packing.

The following day, a Saturday, at an hour when it would still be morning in Cleveland, I set off by streetcar for the distant Central Post and Telegraph Office to begin the complicated, chancy process of telephoning my parents. My excruciating task—which I had hoped to accomplish in good time by a tactfully worded letter—was to convince them that I was okay even though I had decided to leave my husband and besmirch our family record by instigating its first recorded divorce. Tramping the snowy streets, I tried to figure out what on earth to say to protect them from my freedom.

My job was eased by Dr. Hoffman's reassuring report, which he had already cabled to Cleveland: WIFE FINE STOP HUSBAND NEEDS HELP. Nevertheless, Mom's voluble relief upon hearing my voice betrayed the anxiety she was suffering. Finally Dad took the phone. Clearing his throat, he said there was still the . . . er . . . matter of my . . . er . . . pregnancy.

Who was more embarrassed, he or I? Not that I was ashamed or even sorry for my adventure. On the contrary, in those repressive days of entrenched double standards it was so rare for a woman like me to defend free love that having pulled off an entire month of unabashed sexual pleasure as freely as if I were a man gave me a shot of pride undiminished by the looming consequences. But I could hardly explain this to my straitlaced parents, worried sick over me.

First of all, I said, attempting to reassure them, I wasn't sure I was pregnant. And in any case, I was already planning to have a D & C.

In a hospital or an office? asked Dad anxiously. Who would perform it? Would it be legal?

However well meaning these questions, they were precisely what I had hoped to escape by leaving home. To strip them of their secrecy and shame was part of why I became a feminist a decade later, part of why I wrote. My husband's provoking them now was what I could not forgive.

Just as my discomfort was peaking, once again my parents offered to rescue me. Dad wanted me to know that he and Mom had talked it over carefully, and they would be happy to take my baby. They had done it before, they could do it again. They would raise it as their own, no one would have to know, and I would be free to resume my life.

At twenty-four, on the verge of divorce, I had no intention of bearing a child for anyone to raise. Unbeknown to my parents, I'd already had one illegal abortion, and however frightening that experience had been, I was prepared to have another rather than a child. But their incredibly touching offer to take my baby, as Mom's parents had taken in their grandchild Marian, as Mom and Dad had taken in Bob and Johnny, showed me what sort of sacrifice I could count on from them. (In that moment I understood how it might be a sacrifice.) No doubt families can be annoying in every conceivable way. But in extremis mine always came through for me, as I hope, if need be, always to come through for my own.

Preserved in a packet in Mom's drawer were all my cards and letters from that year abroad. Reading them over was almost unbearable to me, so callow, superficial, naive did they seem—reporting on the price of Swiss watches on one page and a visit to Dachau on the next. But there is one letter unlike the rest. No breezy travelogue, it was written after my D & C, from Italy, where, alone for the first time in my life, I began a long painful self-examination. In the letter I try to explain to my worried parents why I can't write them anything but postcards. Reading it over these four decades later, I see it was not their disapproval but their anxiety that oppressed me and sent me into hiding. So anxiously did they wish for my safety that I could tell them nothing but what I thought they wanted to hear. "As I once tried to explain," I wrote in that letter, trying to justify my "reticence,"

I am working very hard at being *absolutely honest* with myself, and you, as intimately interested parties, could only make obstacles for me. Until just now I haven't had any desire or even ability for chit-chat; I've been relentlessly examining, tying loose ends, even mourning unraveled ones; and rather than let dishonesty creep into my mind via cheerful letters to you, I preferred—was compelled—not to write at all. The postcards, inadequate as they seemed to you, cost me dearly: compromise and calculation. And with every urging I received from you, worse, with every hidden sign of your anxiety, the task became more difficult. Once more, then, let me tell you that I am fine and in absolutely no need of worry. I ask you to humor me. Please don't ask for reports. Don't write coy letters, Mother; don't write disgusted ones, Daddy; don't flatter, tease, taunt or cajole; don't organize; don't think ill of me, and for God's sake, don't worry! . . . I have lots and lots to say, but I can't even start as long as I have the hurdle of justification to jump or the burden of explanation to carry. If I told you all my thoughts, I'd have to worry about your feelings. That's really the crux of it: examining my own feelings is as much as I can competently handle now; please don't make me handle yours too. Don't feel obliged (or even inclined, if you can help it) to answer this long-winded missive with a comparable one. Just read it, accept it, and join me in a *silent* understanding. Believe it or not, worrying about *you* has been my largest problem for weeks.

This letter, with its petulant string of don'ts, shows how little I saw my parents as people in their own right rather than merely as family, whose concern I not only took for granted but begrudged. Yet it also shows our anxious regard for one another, even with an ocean between us: they, worrying that their children might take one foolish step and lurch into ruination; we, afraid we might worry them to death.

Back in New York, with my marriage winding down, I found Dad's unsolicited legal advice so burdensome and archaic—insisting, for instance, that I not be seen on a date until my divorce was final—that I resolved to tell my parents nothing. What they didn't know wouldn't hurt them. Just so, it seemed easier not to inform them of my next wedding—a casual event at City Hall—until it was over. By the time Mom's cancer struck a year later, our mutual secrecy was so entrenched that despite Dad's discreet hints, I failed to hear them and attend her.

In her files, attached to a pathologist's report on her tumor, I found a passionate note Mom wrote to Uncle Louis Katz, the eminent doctor, about her "many-prefixed sarcoma," which concludes: "I am told that the additional tissue removed from the leg contained no seedlings. If these reports are true (and I realize that I am surrounded by kindly, well-intentioned liars), then I have not yet lost the fight. Whatever comes, I can take it. I've already had a great deal of happiness and a good life. While I wouldn't mind having more of the same, I'll try to be a good sport in facing whatever is to be. . . . Our real immortality is in our children and I have a fine pair of children who represent my dreams and hopes."

Her dreams and hopes, together with Dad's, had produced the privileges that had set me free. Chasing after a life that might one day make them proud, I had flown so far from her that the dreams and hopes with which she faced a likely death must have been sorely strained when I failed to be at her side—perhaps turning her for a time into one of those same well-intentioned liars she deplored, if only to herself.

*

First thing Monday morning I wheeled each of my parents to the banking office for a final round of signature guarantees. Eager to be relieved of financial responsibility, Dad wanted their remaining assets transferred into my name as trustee. When the banker asked Dad if he knew what he was signing, he gladly told her. But I feared Mom might present a problem. First there was the matter of her signature, which tended to wobble and wander up-up-up off the page. Worse, would she be able to answer the banker's questions? I rehearsed her carefully as we waited our turn. "Mom, the banker will show you this paper and ask if you know what it is. Just say yes. Okay? Then sign it. Now let's rehearse. I'll be the banker."

Each rehearsal was flawless. But when the banker finally asked Mom the question, she forgot her much practiced *yes*. Giving in to the lifelong hostility to authority of so many immigrant families, she fixed the banker with her eye and answered hotly as if insulted, "What do you think I am, an idiot? Of course I know what it is!"

Chapter 11

In the middle drawer of the bureau in the middle bed-room, I came upon a box of presents given to my brother at his thirtieth birthday party: September 7, 1961. They were from his closest friends, our high school crowd, boys I had dated now married to girls I had loved, and each was a joke from a novelty store. A foot-long plastic toothbrush "For Big Mouths" and a matching comb "For Fatheads"; a knitted black cotton tube called a "Bikini for Men"; six knitted coasters in the form of miniature jockstraps and lacy panties; oversized books of matches on their covers printed: "Mabel's House of Ill Fame," "Alcoholics Unanimous," "Alcatraz (on the Rocks)," "The Kremlin, N. Khruschev, Prop., on Salt Mine Drive, Moscow, Russia (Let Us Start a War for You/Wars Started Anywhere)." Each was accompanied by a hu-morous jingle about Bob penned for the occasion, the kind I too had once composed for our high school dances, hayrides, sleigh rides, and sorority rushes.

There was no present from me: I'd left Cleveland nearly a decade before. Had I at least telephoned or sent a card, as Mom must have urged me to do? Perhaps. In 1961, Bob and I were both newly awed by birthdays, the first child of each of us having just been born, and we hadn't yet had our falling out.

I was struck by the affection in those rhymed tributes to Bob, and by how little appeared to have changed from our high school days, despite everyone's having slipped out of their twenties, married, begun families and careers (Bob was selling insurance), and settled into houses a bit farther out in the suburbs than the ones they'd grown up in. It was the height of the postwar boom. No one knew what was coming—the Vietnam War, the New Left, the stepped-up violence against civil rights workers, women's liberation, anything. Yet it was politics that caused our rift a few years later. Race did us in, though given the divergence of our views, it might have been any number of things.

Bob and his wife were visiting New York, spending the weekend with me and my family. I can't remember if it was before or after the summer of their vacation week at Grossinger's, in the Catskills, near enough to New York City that my husband and I drove up one day to join them for dinner. I remember Bob greeting us at the entrance, pulling at his collar, mopping his brow, saying, Boy, are you lucky you came up on Casual Night—otherwise, we'd have to wear jackets and ties, and we'd be really boiling now. I know it was after the summer of the 1963 Civil Rights March on Washington, where my husband and I had gone on a bus with the Seven Arts chapter of CORE (Congress of Racial Equality), a chapter I had named, and heard Martin Luther King, Jr., tell the world his dream. Or maybe it was the summer after that—the New York streets were alive with bongo music that drifted through the windows of our Greenwich Village apartment.

After clearing away the dinner dishes, over coffee my brother and I, seconded by his wife and my husband, foolishly allowed ourselves to fall into a discussion of race. Even though we had both been raised by our ardently liberal parents, I should have known it would end in disaster.

We started out in agreement, repeating the mildest of platitudes—against discrimination and violence, for equality and integration, etc. But before long we lurched into dangerous terrain when Bob drew a line beyond which he "wouldn't want to go." Interracial dating? Mixed neighborhoods? Integrated schools? I don't remember which of those linked issues was primary. Maintaining a soft, reasonable tone with the slightly patronizing cast of an older brother, he illustrated his point with the case of a black friend of his, an athlete I think, perhaps someone he worked with on a community project, whom he liked and had even had to dinner at his house, so couldn't you see he wasn't prejudiced?—but he still wouldn't want that family living on his street because he had a daughter to think about. No, he wouldn't exactly want to have laws about it, that would probably be wrong, but—

At that point, everything heated up. Briefly we went back and forth with arguments, like reasonable people, which we were not, until combustion occurred and then explosion, and I asked him (or, rather, ordered him, shouting) to leave my apartment. If he wouldn't allow a black person to live in his neighborhood, then I wouldn't allow *him* to sleep under my roof—something like that.

Okay, if that's how you feel, said Bob, standing up and signaling his wife, and they got their bags and left and never stayed with me again.

When I asked our mother what Bob had told her about our quarrel and what she thought of it, she said he had reported that we'd been having a discussion when suddenly for no reason I "went crazy," so he didn't hold it against me, and Mom hoped I would forgive him too. After all, she said, he is your brother. And that became the accepted basis of our cool accord, enabling us over the years to maintain a civilized exchange: I was the unpredictably kooky far-left radical from New York who for no discernible reason every so often went a little nuts, but hey, she's my sister. On my side, I thought him a reactionary bigot with whom it would be foolish to discuss politics, without adding the mitigating *but he's my brother.*

How it must have distressed our liberal parents to find themselves squeezed between a conservative Republican who believed blacks and women (including Mom) should stay in their place, and a radical feminist with anarchist leanings who sometimes got arrested. Was their avoidance of political conflict with their children in that era of hot generational strife a testament to their liberal convictions or simple prudence? Johnny does recall a dinner-table debate over Vietnam, with Bob, backed by Dad and Johnny, against me, backed by Mom and Aunt Celia; but by my next visit to Cleveland, Johnny, a physician, was in Vietnam and Dad had switched sides, leaving Bob to defend that war alone.

Mom seemed to have solved the problem of Bob's politics through the useful fog of dementia. "Everyone in our family was a Democrat except my brother Harry," she said one evening when I was visiting Judson. "He was a . . . he was a . . . he was a . . ."

"Republican?" I offered.

"Yes! A Republican! Can you imagine that? A Republican, the rat! And the rest of us all worshiped FDR!"

In her Judson room I had hung a framed photo of the Clintons inscribed "To Dorothy D. Kates, a good friend who has stood behind the Party for many years"—the last of the testaments inscribed by presidents to my ardent mother, who'd attended Kennedy's inaugural ball. As I'd collected movie stars, Mom collected presidents. Most of the children in our school, I recalled, were Republicans, taunting Bob and me with "We Want Wilkie!" and "Dewey for President!" while we fought back bravely for Roosevelt, commander-in-chief of the Armed Forces and friend of the worker, the Negro, and the Jew. But somewhere along the line Bob had flipped over to become deeply conservative—according to certain theories, a standard firstborn, as I am a standard secondborn.

"Wasn't Bob a Republican too?" I ventured.

Mom was shocked. "Our Bob a Republican? Impossible!"

To which Dad replied softly, "I'm afraid you're mistaken there, Bummer."

"How did Bob ever get to be so conservative?" I asked.

"Go on, he never was," said Mom. But Dad shrugged his shoulders and said, "Reaction against the rest of us, I dare say."

＊

Back in New York, every other day I tried to phone Dad not in the evenings when rates were low but in the afternoons, when Mom was wheeled up to his apartment and I could talk to them both. There was so much I wanted to know.

One afternoon, pencil poised, I asked them what they were proudest of in their lives and was astonished when Dad came back with his academic rankings of seventy years before: magna cum laude in law school and second out of six hundred on the state bar exam—"beaten out for first by a woman, you'll be glad to know."

The pride of his life an academic record! Among the select papers he had saved from his youth, I found the newspaper clippings announcing his scores along with yellowed telegrams and letters of congratulations. In his memoir he recorded that after the bar exam scores had been published in the newspaper, his grammar school principal, Miss Rose McCourt, remembering him "as an assiduous library attendant and conscientious student," had come downtown to his office personally to shake his hand.

No wonder that Bob, a mediocre student, had often felt squeezed, picked on, undervalued, misunderstood. No wonder he resented me, his nemesis, who, he accused, was able to get away with murder because I sometimes aced my courses.

"But Daddy," I said, "you're ninety-four years old. You took those exams seventy years ago. There must have been other things since then that meant more to you. Forget proudest. What did you most *value* in your life?"

"My work," he snapped back without a moment's hesitation. "I loved my work." Not trial work, which he found impossibly stressful since the outcome hinged on his performance (he'd thrown up each night of the one murder trial he'd undertaken, knowing a man's life was at stake), but arbitration work, where others presented the arguments and he had only to render judgment. His four thousand written decisions involved almost every kind of employer and union, public and private, from all over the country, and he prided himself on being invited back to the same factories repeatedly. Once when he refused to hear a case because he had a cousin in management, the union wanted him anyway. (Dad still declined.)

Given our father's devotion to justice, how Bob's repeated charge of unfairness must have wounded him. "I'm afraid Bob was often dissatisfied with me," he confessed sorrowfully.

Was it true? I didn't know. Bob was certainly a dutiful son, if often an overbearing one, but dissatisfied? Mom once told me that Dad thought I hated him because of my intolerant complaints about his incessant annoying drummings and tappings of his fingers and feet. He can't help it, she said protectively, that's just the way Sam is, it's physical, built right into his system. I was stricken to learn that he should think I hated him. I admit I hated his nervous tapping, but hate *him*? How could he believe such a thing! I couldn't tell if such disastrous misunderstanding was due to my lack of or Dad's excess of sensitivity. And if I couldn't tell in my own case, I certainly couldn't tell in Bob's.

"Why do you think he was dissatisfied with you?" I asked.

"Because of my relationship with you. He thought we favored you."

"Did you?"

"*I* certainly didn't think so. Nevertheless, he was jealous of you."

"When did it start?"

"At a very early age."

"Why?"

"Primarily because of your school marks."

Bob's report cards, nestled in the drawer, showed his teachers' alarms from early on. "Bobby should try to overcome nail-biting and thumb-sucking"; "written work is carelessly done"; "untidy and inaccurate"; "it will probably be necessary to have regular reading periods at home"; "Bob's reading is his greatest handicap." Still, by high school his grades, from an era when C really meant average, show Bob an average student, seldom excelling but not in serious danger of failure either, especially given that every Ohio public university, our presumed destination, accepted all graduates of Ohio high schools. True, my grades, though not stupendous, were uniformly better than Bob's; but to hear our father worry, you'd think they were our defining difference.

Reading Bob's letters home from college, where he was studying business administration, brought his troubles tumbling back. After his routine requests for money ("My fine, aging, rich father: Would you kindly deposit $250 in my account to pay my house bill. Your aging, penniless son") and services ("Mother, please send my clean laundry to me in some small box from home as it will be hard to send you my laundry box now that my old laundry occupies it." Or: "Where are all those baked goods you promised to send me?"); behind his reports on social life ("A big weekend is approaching. It looks as if I will be at three all-night parties") and fortuitous pleasures ("Yesterday I accidentally got into a crap game. I passed 13 times and ended up winning $40") lie periodic confessions that his grades are "too poor to mention," followed by the inevitable promise to improve ("This weekend I am going to turn into a bookworm. Don't worry"). The parental urgings to which he responded survive in but a single letter to Bob from Dad, accompanying a deposit slip on the National City Bank of Cleveland for $530: "I hope you had a lovely New Year in every way. Be sure to buckle down to work. I was happy with your grades and hope you keep up the good work. With loads of love, Dad."

In the Air Force following college Bob seemed to come into his own, setting firm parental limits: "I want to be on record that when I am home on leave I am in the category of a guest, and that completely excludes me from having to entertain other guests." After asking Mom to check out car prices "on either a 1955 Buick Special convertible, a 1955 Buick Century convertible, or any other 1955 convertible such as a Mercury or Pontiac," he cautions her, "Please don't write and lecture me on the idea of not buying now, as I do realize all the advantages and shortcomings." He could also be reassuring ("Mother—don't panic so easily. It's a big world with lots of opportunities"), even profusely appreciative ("Thanks for a wonderful party. Your love and kindness are two gifts I'll treasure for the rest of my life").

Then why were our parents so concerned? Was it ordinary middle-class anxiety that made them fear Bob would fail to make his way, as they feared I might never stay out of trouble?

Though I kept pressing my questions, Dad was evasive. When I asked what Bob most cared about in life, he suggested I ask Mom.

"I'm asking *you,* Daddy."

"In my opinion," said my humble father, who seldom asserted but often opined—"in my opinion he was interested in sports and his friends. In college he was some sort of referee, and he was business manager of the high school football team, you know."

Yes, I knew. Bob had settled for business manager when he failed to make the team. (My boyfriend was a quarterback.) It was around then that his friends began calling him "Whoopsie"—whether with affection or derision I couldn't tell, though the one time I used the name myself, Bob smacked me. No more than I could fathom what underlay the F.A. Club he founded—the Fuck Alix Club, that spread through our crowd like whooping cough one semester. When I heard about it well into the epidemic, I was shaken. Bewildered, hurt, but also scared. Was it a nasty joke I could ignore, or were there sexual overtones that might have consequences? I needed to know the purpose of the club, who belonged, how one became a member—but to ask was to acknowledge its existence and Bob's betrayal. Nor could I tell our parents—Bob was safe there—since they would have been horrified by the *F*-word and its implications. In the end, I took the high road of patronizing my brother by ignoring his club.

"How would you describe Bob—angry? contented? ambitious? what?" I asked.

"I'd say he was mostly contented, wouldn't you, Bummer?" Dad asked Mom.

"What?" she said. "Who?"

"Alix is asking about Bob. She wants to know what he most cared about."

"What Bob wanted in his life," said Mom decisively, "was to be successful. And he was."

Successful—a word I would never have associated with Bob. Was this another bit of Mom's self-delusion? Or perhaps, I suddenly thought, it was my observation, my presence, that tainted Bob's success, like some perverse scientific effect, some Uncertainty Principle of the heart. Maybe I couldn't see what others saw because of my evil eye.

There was evidence enough of Bob's success: those affectionate jingles from his thirtieth birthday; the Million Dollar Round Table, awarded for selling a million dollars of life insurance in a single year; and most memorably his funeral, where for a moment I glimpsed his life as he would have wanted me to. The chapel packed with mourners—all the friends from our youth and scores of people I'd never met—was a resounding testament to his success. The eulogy praised him as a rock of the Jewish community: an active member of his temple, B'nai B'rith, and the Jewish Community Center where he was a board member and led classes in physical fitness until he lost his own. A Masonic honor guard from his lodge in full regalia formed a canopy of crossed swords for the casket of their "Worshipful Brother" to pass beneath, and a row of buglers paid mournful tribute. As the hearse and its entourage drove slowly through the wealthy Cleveland suburb of Beachwood past Beachwood City Hall, I saw that the flag was lowered to half mast and the steps were lined with office workers paying their respects. For four years Bob had sat on the city council, following twelve years on the school board, including two terms as board president—all elected offices—and had once been chosen Beachwood Man of the Year. ("I'm afraid I sold Bob short in the leadership department," Dad said to me one night. "How do you mean?" I asked. He shook his head. "I had no confidence he could become a community leader. But he did.") His obituary quoted Bob's widow as saying, "He was very education-oriented. He believed in it for himself. He had two degrees"—the first a bachelor's in business from Ohio State, the second a master's in financial services from American College. Throughout the 1970s while I was writing feminist books and committing civil disobedience, Bob was sitting on the Beachwood school board still stretching the boundaries of the good. Now I wondered if his belated educational efforts that made it into the very headline of his obituary (ROBERT D. KATES, WAS EDUCATION-ORIENTED) had finally won him the approval he longed for from Dad.

Until I read Bob's obituary, I had forgotten that he took his master's degree in the same year I took mine, 1979. In my patronizing way—my idea of sisterly—I'd enlisted our parents to keep mine secret from Bob for fear of diminishing the value of his. Perhaps I was only following their own example, set back in our childhood, when they told us I had skipped 3B not because of my schoolwork but because our class was overcrowded. Explaining their fib years later, they said they hadn't wanted me to get "a swelled head," but it may really have been to comfort Bob, whose chief advantage over me in school was rapidly, visibly diminishing.

*

My brother and I were rivals as children, adversaries as teens, and strangers as adults, maintaining at best a sullen standoff. I don't recall our ever having been allies. Not once do I remember either of us seeking refuge or help from the other; if we offered each other help, it was because Mom asked us to, and we gave it grudgingly. I mastered the slip and goad, Bob the punch and shout.

Yet when I quizzed Mom about Bob, she maintained that he always had great affection and respect for me.

"How can you say that?" I said. "He wouldn't even let his children visit us in New York."

"Oh, go on!" she said.

"Really. He wouldn't," I said, beginning to feel defensive. "He thought Manhattan was a dangerous place and didn't trust me to protect them."

But Mom continued to insist that, on the contrary, Bob was proud of my accomplishments and hurt when I failed to reciprocate.

I wondered why she was taking his side, forcing me to marshall evidence. "That's not the way I remember it," I began. "First of all . . ."

Mom raised her hand and interrupted me. Leaving diplomacy aside she set her voice at its most emphatic pitch and announced, "You don't have to remember, Alix. It's enough that it's true."

I lacked the heart to argue. Could she be right? Could I, not she, have misread Bob? Whatever the facts, I had to admire my resourceful mother who had just neatly adapted to the limitations of dementia by switching the very grounds of conviction from *memory,* which could fail her, to *truth,* which could not. Adapter to the end.

Chapter 12

With the house finally on the market I had to decide what to keep, what to donate, what to sell, what to auction, and how to divide up the keepsakes. Anything I did not personally dispose of would go to the liquidators, and after that the buyout man would give the house its final sweep, hauling away whatever remained, from my grandmother's furniture in the servants' suite where she'd ended her century of life, to the ancient window shades and broken flowerpots, down to the last mote of family dust.

In the delicate matter of who took what, I kept consulting Bob's daughter, Lisa, the grandchild most devoted to my parents. Without the competitive edge Bob and I would have felt, we declared our desires—she for herself and her brother, I for me and my children—in hurried meetings in Cleveland and phone calls from New York. Living in suburban Chicago, Lisa and her brother had room for such substantial items as a dining table, dressers, and a desk, whereas my children and I, apartment dwellers all, could use only smaller pieces. I was content; what mattered most to me was the priceless record of my parents' aspirations, disappointments, and achievements.

Dad's achievement was public, preserved in those four

thousand arbitration decisions at the Ohio Historical Society; Mom's was harder to know. Both she and Dad believed in self-creation, perhaps the bedrock of their marriage, but it had always been harder for her than for him to fashion a reliable self. His law degree conferred a mandate and an income, whereas she had to rely on ingenuity and will. Though these qualities were enhanced by the privileges of education, charm, and her husband's position, they couldn't easily get her where she wanted to go. Had she been forced by necessity or born later, she might have consolidated her skills into a single concentrated career instead of putting together an eight-course banquet of a self, composed of family, politics, travel, romance, music, writing, art, and ceaseless education. But not there, not then.

Finding in her files the evidence of her activities, I was struck by my ignorance and, worse, my dismissal of her work. Not since I was an adoring child had I acknowledged it. Feminism had cured me of the culture's disregard of women's unpaid and unappreciated labors, firing me to write about homemakers, mothers, domestics, clericals, and prostitutes, all demeaned and exploited for their (our) services. Once I understood how unjustly *they make you do it then blame you for it,* I spent the rest of my life furiously writing books and essays to expose the scam. But when it came to the "volunteer" labor of "privileged" women like Mom, I'd blindly shared the cultural prejudice that condemned it as marginal, frivolous, self-serving—not in the same league with the serious work of men like Dad.

Confronted by the proof of her varied and passionate efforts, I had to rethink my presumptions. Frivolous? Self-serving? Not in face of those hundreds of suburban women listed in her files whom she organized for Kennedy in 1959, following her radiation therapy, and again for Johnson,

Carter, Mondale, Eugene McCarthy, Clinton. Not her campaign against racist blockbusting in Shaker Heights, acknowledged in a letter from Cleveland's mayor Carl Stokes, first black mayor of a major U.S. city. Not in the view of the cancer patients whom Mom coached in her singular self-help method of fighting back. Not according to the local artists for whom she mounted exhibitions at the Women's City Club. And even her ceaseless efforts at self-improvement embodied more vitality and hope than frivolity. Here were notes for all her studies, from current history, modern art, and new music, to Japanese tea ceremonies, Chinese cooking, contemporary Persian. Dog-eared copies of *How to Travel Without Being Rich* and *Where to Vacation on a Shoestring.* Detailed journals of all the trips she and Dad ever took—to Europe, the Middle East, the Far East—and one of the monthlong journey she took by herself at seventy, without companion or group, to visit ashrams and refugee camps in India and Pakistan, after Dad swore off traveling. He was given to such renunciations, but until Bob died, she never renounced a thing: "I rallied my antibodies to fight off the invader," she wrote of her cancer. "Deep within me I believed in my life."

Alongside her hopes was also the record of her disappointments. Beginning with her writing. On the eve of publication of my first novel at thirty-nine, my mother, sixty-four, wrote to me: "When I was about your age I remember thinking that if I didn't start something career-wise before 40 I would never make it. I didn't and so didn't. *You did!* And what wonderful children too."

I vaguely remembered that she had written when I was a child, but I had little notion of what. Here were manuscripts from the early 1930s of short stories, one-act plays, historical essays, even three chapters of a family novel penned on Dad's obsolete stationery in that hand so like my own. There were pieces about marital compromise, a homosexual cousin, a syphilitic brother, a bored young wife, a philandering husband. There were vignettes of Depression woe about itinerant laborers, immigrant peasants, the injured, the unemployed. And as Cleveland hurtled toward war, she came up with a series of articles, tentatively titled "Once Again," comparing current events with their historical precedents, of which she had completed three sample manuscripts. When these works were rejected (all were rejected) and the war was over, undaunted, she took another tack, writing two courtroom series for radio, earnest and edifying: one of Supreme Court cases, another called *Arbitration on the Air,* cases courtesy of Dad.

As I read those scripts of half a century ago, typed by Dad in triplicate on crisp onionskin, the excitement of Mom's brief media career knocked open my memory. The crackle of those pages put me back in the small Ashurst study where, returning from school, I always found Mom seated at a desk piled high with documents and legal pads, a lipsticked cigarette or coffee cup in one hand, pencil in the other. The air was filled with the furious energy of her ambition which, once I launched my own life, I somehow forgot. Why? Did I find her endeavors insignificant or her disappointment unbearable? The whole family had colluded in that exhilarating fantasy—Dad typing each revision, and the rest of us, her children, parents, sisters, providing the dazzled audience for her dramatic readings of each script, from the announcer's introduction right down to the three closing gavel thumps made by Mom's fist over her piano simulation of a martial band. After so many revisions, rehearsals, and hopes, after the flurry of letters and telegrams to network executives setting up appointments in New York City, preserved like pressed flowers in a Hotel New Yorker envelope along with train tickets, telephone numbers, and restaurant receipts from April 1947, just as Mom turned forty, how bitter must have tasted the rejections, one on top of another, from all three major networks and several unions. *If I didn't start something career-wise before 40 I would never make it.* For the next quarter century she stopped writing.

It was the sense of my mother's circumscribed possibilities and thwarted ambitions, however unacknowledged, that sent me, like so many feminists of my class and generation, reeling headlong into the movement. It was to avoid her fate (and keep my birthright) that I'd vowed to remain forever childless—only to change my mind and have a child on the eve of thirty, then considered the last safe moment to begin a family. Consoled by the enchantment of my children—a boy and a girl—I threw myself fervently into the tasks of motherhood, for which I'd quit my editorial job, accepting the alarming isolation that followed like a good sport. (Or like my mother, that consummate good sport.) Having freely chosen motherhood, I considered it demeaning to complain, though I had my secret thoughts. Tied down at home by two babies, with a philandering husband and only the occasional freelance job to keep alive some glimmer of the life of significance or purpose to which I'd once aspired, I was a perfect candidate for the nascent women's liberation movement.

By the time I discovered the movement at thirty-five, Mom was in her sixties and no less eager to be shaken up than I was. Just as I began writing in the wake of feminism, so did she. At sixty-five, months after my first novel was published, she completed a moving essay about my grandmother's death, which was quickly placed in a national magazine. I presumed my writing had inspired hers. Another essay, "I Was Given a Year to Live," detailing her successful battle with cancer, was accepted for an anthology. A third essay, called "Women's Liberation in Moscow," found no publisher, but so what? By then Mom was studying Persian in preparation for writing a novel, to be set in the fictional country of Trislayistan, loosely fashioned after Afghanistan, with a plot of international intrigue and intercultural romance, inspired by the story of one of Dad's relations and his Japanese war bride. Since her mid-fifties Mom had been seriously studying French: there in her files to prove it were her college transcripts, with a cumulative 4-point average; several hundred annotated volumes of French classics, novels, poems, and essays spilling out of her bedroom bookshelves; and a plaque from Le Cercle des Conférences Françaises with whom she met to speak French every month for three decades. So Persian didn't daunt her. "I am starting a novel which I am quite excited about," she wrote to an editor. "It is to be set in the Orient where I am going in mid-April. It's great to be writing again!"

Confronted by such incontestable evidence of Mom's serious literary aspirations going all the way back to my early childhood, I had to ask myself why it had never occurred to me to attribute my ambition to hers, rather than hers to mine. Why, in the secret story of my life, did I trace my vocation to the example and support of my father, who typed my papers and corrected my mistakes, though Mom was the English teacher; or ascribe it to my love of books, for which I also credited Dad, my literary guide and discussant, despite the lingering image of Mom lying on the living room sofa night after night, long after the rest of us had gone to bed, engrossed in massive contemporary tomes from Winston Churchill's memoirs to Whittaker Chambers's *Witness;* or to a high school English teacher's exacting standards; or to my first husband's attempts at fiction; or to my editorial jobs; or to the well-known writer my second husband brought home to live with us for a month (*if that's how it's done,* I thought, *I can too!*); or to the examples of Grace Paley and Tillie Olsen, whose mind-expanding stories about young urban mothers changed my idea of literature; or to the women's liberation movement; or even to human nature—but never to my mother. Nor did I connect her reform liberal activism, which dotted my childhood with moments of vicarious glory, to my own radical feminist activism. Rather, blindly succumbing to the very sexism I'd thought I had fashioned my life to overthrow, I'd defined her chiefly by her maternal sacrifice, smearing her worldly accomplishments with the demeaning epithets "dabbler," "amateur," "volunteer," "suburban"—as if my own ambition and engagement were paid in some more valuable currency than hers.

Carolyn Heilbrun writes of the "powerful enigma" that is a woman's—especially a feminist woman's—need "to separate from her mother to the point of making her an enemy." Living a world-plus-three-hundred-miles away from mine, effectively banishing her from my life, I did not need to make her my enemy. But, nearly as cruelly, I failed to acknowledge my ties to her or her effect upon me until it was nearly too late. Those ties had once been so tight that to honor them, or even acknowledge them, was to risk being hobbled by them. Only after I had made my way in a world that excluded her did they begin to seem benign.

Not even the birth of my own children in the early 1960s gave me access to her feelings. True, possessed by motherhood and reimmersed in the stream of generations, I felt a new kinship with my parents. Our shared preoccupation with my children increased the traffic between us, occasioning volleys of letters and providing dependable subject matter for our sporadic conversations. I began to welcome their phone calls. But so seldom did I pick up the phone to call them that after years of forbearance Dad—who from the time he married had tried to speak to his mother every day—blurted out to me, "Why is it that we only hear from you when you want something?"

The question hit me like a hurled rock. The fact was, it never occurred to me to call them except for a purpose. Not that I thought of them unfeelingly but, more careless than cruel, I forgot to think of them.

Stung by Dad's rebuke, I imagined my mother, hurt but vigilant, begging him to suppress it, and after weighing the pros and cons adamantly refusing: *No, Bummer. I've made up my mind. The next time she calls I'm going to say something.*

After that I tried to phone them whenever I had good news. Disturbing news, bound to upset them, like my already troubled second marriage, I continued to suppress. But from then on I doubled my efforts to remember their birthdays, though sometimes with limited success.

By the time Mom was ready at sixty-six to tackle a novel again, I was teaching writing workshops at New York University. This afforded me the ironic satisfaction of offering her tips on organization and discipline, as if she were not my mother but my student ("My secret," I wrote to her, "is to make a detailed outline and work every day"), and prompted Dad to confess to me his concern for Mom's failure of will. I know she wants to write this book, he told me, and I remind her daily, but for some reason she doesn't seem able to do it.

I, published expert, cautioned him that his very re-minders brought an intolerable pressure bound to be coun-terproductive.

Even from me? he asked, amazed.

Especially from you, Daddy!

Reading over my mother's works, I am struck by one gap-ing absence. She wrote from many points of view: histo-rian, politico, wife, daughter, cancer survivor—but not as a mother. Except for one story from the 1930s about a young married couple whose baby ties the wife down, and a later one about the troubled child next door, she never wrote about children or motherhood. In her eighties, after Bob died, she planned to write about him, but she didn't get around to it.

Until I began this book, I thought motherhood might have been just too complex or painful a subject for Mom to tackle. Or, alternatively, I conjectured that her children were not, as she insisted, the sum and center of her life after all. Now I believe she was honoring a taboo. If what she had to say could conceivably hurt her children, she'd bite off her tongue before risking it. Even feminist mothers for whom the subject of motherhood is a passion seldom write candidly about it except abstractly or from the point of view of a daughter. This leaves a great hole in our knowledge that few are willing to fill. Certainly not I. Though the sub-ject of my life as a mother could be another chapter in this book, like my own mother, I remain silent.

*

I was drinking espresso with my friend Paula in an outdoor café on Fourth Street in Greenwich Village. New York's brief spring was late: while youths on Rollerblades paraded new outrageous hairdos, we huddled inside our coats. Soon I'd be leaving for the island—for how long, I didn't know. With my parents increasingly vulnerable I was making few plans. Part of me thought I ought to stay close to a phone and an airport. But, craving the solitude I needed to work on my book after the upheavals of the winter, I decided to risk the distance, resolving to somehow phone Judson daily and be ready to fly to Cleveland on a day's notice.

Though old friends, lately Paula and I had only one topic: parents. Paula had just returned from an abrupt trip to Florida to calm down the woman who cared for her ailing mother, ten years a widow. "This is the fourth person this year. We've lost so many good people. They stay a few months and then quit," she lamented.

"Why?"

"Why! Mother is impossible. She can't be left alone, but she drives her caregivers mad. I don't know what we'll do if this woman leaves. I offered her a substantial raise if she'll stay till the end of the year. My sister lives in Denver, I'm in New York. We can't fly down there every week to deal with each new crisis."

"What will you do at the end of the year?" I asked.

She stared into her coffee cup. "If this doesn't work out, I'm afraid we'll have to find a home for her. She says she'll never go, but she won't do anything to avoid it. I don't want it either, but what can we do? I can't bring her here. She's too impossible. She always was. And on top of everything else, she's losing her sight."

Her sight! Poor Paula! I thought, glad that aside from Dad's deafness and Mom's Alzheimer's, my parents had all their senses.

After telling her all I knew about nursing homes, it was my turn to unburden myself. What was getting me down today, I said, wasn't my parents—they were okay—but my own filial failings.

Paula laughed and shook her head. "What nonsense! Just think of the *naches* you've given your parents all these years."

"*Naches?*" I asked sheepishly.

"You don't know that word? It's Yiddish for . . . *pride.*"

"Oh. Then I'm not so sure," I demurred. "My two divorces, my politics . . . Remember, they're from Cleveland."

"Come on. Think about it. All those books you've written."

Paula's certainty buoyed me. Could she be right? Could *naches* outweigh neglect? Perhaps. I couldn't deny that despite the sex in my novels, my straitlaced parents were my most ardent fans, showering copies of my books on all their relatives and friends, as if the promise I'd realized was their own.

When I began writing, I'd been so apprehensive about their responses to my work that I pretended they would never read me. But after reading my first novel, Dad wrote, "Even my normal 'square' outlook was not greatly upset by your sometimes earthy language, nor by the descriptions of private thoughts and actions which in my younger days were omitted from books of general circulation. Times certainly are different!" Although, of a later novel of mine he admitted, "As you told Dorothy you anticipated, I found the detailed descriptions of sexual activity somewhat objectionable." Yet he ended that very letter with praises that vindicated my hopes and purred in my heart: "For style, imagery, insight, analysis, emotion, and the general beautiful use of the English language, I found the book superb. You are a remarkably splendid writer in my opinion, and you again have made me very proud." I remembered how nervously I'd watched him read the galleys of my second novel on my green velvet sofa in New York, and how I melted when, as he came to the part where the teen-aged heroine leaves home (a crucial scene in all my books), he pulled out his large hanky to dry his eyes as he'd always done when he was moved.

Mom outdid him, reading my story as her own. "I am thrilled with your book, which I have read and reread," she wrote of the very book Dad had found "somewhat objectionable." "How well you understand marriage and family and separately the need for sexual adventure and love," she continued, as if I had taken her side in their private quarrel. "Your novel is a reflection of family life held together by a nurturing mother who, like her striving children, must find fulfillment outside the family restrictions."

Having publicly violated the prim sexual silence that governed our family, our community, our time, I was relieved to see the threat of disgrace that had chased me from home and sealed our lips for decades finally begin to dissolve. (Oh, the liberating return of the repressed!) Mom took my fictional revelations as an invitation to confide her own secrets, and for the first time in decades we spoke as intimates, whispering giddily over the teacups.

The feminism that inspired my books not only opened channels between us but gave me something to offer back. With the advent of the movement I finally began to take notice of my mother, viewing her life, like my own, in that penetrating light. I took an interest in her writing, sent her to my agent and my editor, and to her surprised delight, pressed her rights against Dad:

Why should you do all the cooking? I challenged, as she moved toward the kitchen from the living room, where we three had been immersed in conversation all afternoon. Or all the housework either. It's Dad's house too. Actually, he's the big eater. You're as busy as he is. Why must it all fall to you?

Mom was tickled. At dinner that night, after Bob and his family had joined us, she repeated my charges, teasing, Well, Sammy, and what have you to say in your defense? Not that she'd ever complained about the division of household labor. For all her striving toward modernity she was solidly of her time and class. But if this was the gift her daughter proffered, she would embrace it. As she often said, beggars can't be choosers.

Bob thought my meddling not only kooky but dangerous; now when he laughed at my ideas, his laughter had a nervous edge. But Dad judiciously considered my harangue. Instead of upsetting him, it seemed to energize him, as if my pugnacious challenge was merely an extension of our long adversarial tango. Was he secretly proud of my politics? In a letter to me about an unsolicited red-bordered "Kates coat of arms" and "historiography" he'd received in the mail, he wrote, "You may find the enclosed reference to the Kates name origins of interest if not amusement. Although I am one of the less militant Kateses, the warrior strain has emerged in my daughter." (In his memoir Dad wrote of his own involvement with politics: "While a stenographer at General Electric and later I read books on socialism, including Bellamy's *Looking Backward*. As a result, when Norman Thomas ran for president of the United States, I wrote to him offering to campaign for him. I received no reply, and that ended my radical career. . . . As a young lawyer, I felt that getting into politics was one way to further my career. I joined the Democratic party and made speeches for Franklin Roosevelt and local candidates.

Later, in 1938, a lawyer who was the Democratic ward leader where I then lived asked me to run for precinct committeeman in my precinct. He assured me that all I needed to do was to get five signatures on a nominating petition, that I would have no opposition, and that I would not need to do any campaigning. However, an opposing candidate filed at the last moment, campaigned vigorously, and won the election. That was the end of my political career.")

Though already seventy, by my next visit to Cleveland he was pleased to report he had assumed all dishwashing chores. He began to substitute the unwieldy locution *he-or-she* for the universal *he,* and as the years went by he gradually took over more and more of the domestic duties left undone by the weekly cleaning woman until, upon his retirement, he was in charge of all the shopping, cooking, serving, dishwashing, laundry, bills, and, after Mom began to lose her bearings, even driving. He never stopped calling women *girls,* and he staunchly clung to the niceties of gendered manners: he'd open doors for women, hold their coats, walk curbside, pay up. But even as he tipped his hat to the ladies, he cut a new swath along a new path.

*

Within weeks of the realtor's spring Open House, after a few desultory nibbles, we landed a buyer—a single doctor from England who would be moving to town in the fall to head a department at the renowned Cleveland Clinic. Our realtor thought him an ideal catch since the Clinic was willing to underwrite his mortgage. I was relieved to have the entire summer before vacating my parents' house. The truth was, I had begun to relish inhabiting it—and them—after so many years of standing apart. As each new parental crisis brought me back to Cleveland, I indulged my fantasies by playing house ever more boldly. When I slipped into Mom's clothes, drank tea from her porcelain cups, greedily read the spines of my father's books and dipped into the magical texts that returned me to childhood, or even when I simply used Mom's notepaper, sat at Dad's desk, or drove their car to Judson, I felt the tingle of a healing wound, the balm of reconciliation.

It must have been hard on my parents to see their home go to a stranger. Yet, in the months between contract and closing, Dad, elated by the price we got but convinced the doctor would change his mind (what would a single man want with all those rooms?), worried himself sleepless that the sale would fall through. Though it had been three years since his last arbitration hearing and many more since he'd practiced general law, Dad spent his nights rereading the documents for loopholes and recalculating the numbers.

Mom had a different concern. "That Englishman who's going to reside in our house. I don't know him, but maybe we'll be friends. Tell me frankly," she said, speaking low, "do you think the English are standoffish or friendly? Not that I expect to be friends with him; I have my friends."

"Mom, it depends on the Englishman. He's coming to head a department at the Clinic, so he's going to be very busy. And he's young. A bachelor. He may be looking for a mate."

Mom pushed back her silky dark hair that still had only a few wisps of grey and said with a coquettish toss of her head, "I don't qualify."

"Right, Mom," I said, "you're already married"—impressed anew by the persistence of character that not even the vagaries of dementia could unseat.

Chapter 13

Judson's residents being overwhelmingly Christian, I was surprised to see nearly forty people gathered in the auditorium as my husband and I wheeled my parents in for the Passover seder. Six large tables were festively set with candles, wineglasses, and plates piled high with matzoh. We sat at a table with another resident from five and her daughter Terry and her granddaughter Diana.

As the men donned yarmulkes and the candles were lit, I realized that not since my childhood had I been to a seder with my parents. Except for Bob, we were all non-believers. I remembered the distant seders at our grandparents' houses: First Seder at the Davises, with Bob, Johnny, and me crawling around under the table untying everyone's shoelaces; Second Seder at the Kateses, with a separate children's table for all the giggling cousins. The scenes rushed back with the prayers and songs led by a rabbi Judson snagged for the occasion and a young cantor with blond ponytail and beard who circulated among the tables strumming a guitar.

To accommodate the residents' short attention spans the service was brief; even so, some people ate the ceremonial foods and wine as if they were the meal. Mom so enjoyed the *haroset*—a concoction of chopped apples, cinnamon, walnuts, and red wine meant to symbolize the mortar used by the enslaved ancient Jews in building cities for their Egyptian captors—that instead of passing the dish for all to sample she kept it to herself, polishing it off with her fingers after dropping the spoon.

Suddenly, during the Four Questions the other resident at our table began to weep and wail. Terry apologized, explaining to us that her mother was grieving for her own long-dead mother.

"When did she die?" asked Dad.

"Oh, fifty years ago."

For some reason Mom found this amusing. Every few minutes she leaned over to me on her left, then to my husband on her right, to exclaim with a chuckle, "Imagine that!—that grandma is mourning her mother who died fifty years ago."

When the food arrived, the weeping woman sat before her matzoh-ball soup and roast chicken with clenched teeth. The more Terry urged her to eat, the louder she refused, sometimes addressing her daughter as Mama, as if she herself were young and her daughter middle-aged.

"At the Chanukah party four months ago she was as fine as your mother," Terry confided to me. "But now half the time she doesn't know me. She barely eats and she often cries."

In a mere four months? I was shocked. "How old is she?"

"Ninety-one. And your mother?"

"Eighty-eight," I whispered.

"Eighty-eight! Really! I thought she was in her seventies."

On my other side Mom periodically pulled my sleeve and repeated in my ear with a snicker, "That grandma is mourning her mother who died fifty years ago"—until

Dad said, "You know, Bummer, one can mourn for someone no matter when they may have died." Then Mom turned sad, and I thought of Bob.

When the wails at our table began to draw stares, Terry wheeled her mother out. Immediately the atmosphere lightened. With the help of song sheets and guitar the cantor led us through the familiar Passover songs—"One Only Kid," "Who Knows One," "Dayenu." Dad sang melody while Mom hummed harmony.

After their own parents died, my atheist parents dispensed with seders altogether, only resuming the practice in deference to Bob, who from his bar mitzvah on had grown increasingly observant, even fasting on Yom Kippur.

"Do you think Bob was really religious or only observed the forms?" I asked when the singing had died down.

"I presume he was a true believer," said Dad.

In our freethinking house religious belief was heretical; now I wondered if Bob, like me, had enjoyed his rebellion. I never took his seriously, never called him for the holidays or sent him a card—only sometimes a picture postcard from abroad and the obligatory souvenir. (But nothing like those I sent our parents. There they all were in the house, waiting for me to reclaim them: the earrings and scarves, the neckties and chess set, the cups and lacquerware I sent home from my travels in place of myself.) Mostly I forgot I had a brother once I left Cleveland. He was an afterthought. Why don't you give Bob a call? Dad would suggest soon after I arrived for one of my rare visits. Don't worry, I said, I will after dinner. But sometimes I forgot. No wonder Mom had to write to me, "As you know, on September 7 Bob will be 40. It has significance to him, so if you will, it would be nice to write him or call him."

If you will.

Does it never end?

It ends. My brother died.

But first, he was dying, as our mother, sobbing, informed me by phone.

He was afraid to die; he proclaimed it willingly, even proudly. If I'm dying, he said, I don't want to know. I don't want to die. I'm so afraid.

This fear made him brave. For two years bravely he fought his cancer. I'm going to lick it, he said. I intend to fight this and win. They say fifteen percent survive. I'm going to be in that fifteen percent.

And for a while he seemed to be winning as he defiantly lived on past the doctors' predictions by half a year, a year, a year and a half. Chortling, he'd take his chemo gratefully, accepting the ambiguous results of each new lung scan. A challenge. One thing about me, he said, I've never been a quitter. To underscore his confidence he sold his four-bedroom suburban house and moved into a sexy condo with a cathedral ceiling in a gated community complete with clubhouse, tennis courts, a lake with ducks. He started throwing large parties, undertook unprecedented trips.

I was amazed. Was this my brother? The one who always threatened to tell, who gave up more and more easily when I set out to best him? Till then he'd never ventured farther from Cleveland than Florida; now suddenly: Israel, Europe! Who was this new trend-setting brother, this fighter? Never before had I seen him in that light, though perhaps had I cared to look I might have. Had he changed? Or had he come out of hiding? Or was I the one who was changing or coming out of hiding?

His daughter, Lisa, was engaged. Everyone was so glad for him, hoped he might live to see her married. (Knock on wood.) Big white wedding, more religious than we would have thought, champagne, dancing, ancient relatives, all the out-of-town cousins. Bob choked up giving his daughter away, and again at the first toast. Everyone exchanged knowing glances, everyone in the know. He raised his glass and said, I'm so happy to see Lisa and Joe married, I can't tell you folks. This makes me a happy man. He blinked back his tears while smiling a big sniffly grin. He pulled out a large white handkerchief—just like Dad when he was moved. People grinned and danced. Our parents danced.

My brother, still handsome despite the surgery, the chemo, the radiation, praised his son (looking just like Bob in his youth only taller, handsomer) for his success as a salesman. Only two years out of Michigan, he won a two-week paid vacation to Hawaii for two—that big a salesman. I'm so happy, proclaimed my brother at the wedding, I'm going to live to see Adam do five million. Mark my words.

Secretly, I thought he was foolish to hope—until he started to win. As each scan remained clean, I came to admire his battle (it cost me nothing), though I didn't think about him very often, except when there was some change, some "news." I mainly phoned our parents, not Bob, for news, and tried to comfort them. But after the shadow appeared on his second lung, I vowed to make up for the years we were strangers, in the same spirit in which I'd vowed in elementary school to listen to the war news on a portable radio during recess. Seeking virtue. Failing. "I can't thank you enough for your caring and concern during the ordeal of the last three weeks. Your calls were so important and deeply appreciated," he wrote to me. "Honey, you were terrific and it is hard to express in words how important it is to know that those close to you really care." But I knew my response was inadequate.

Then he took a bad turn. The shadow spread to two ribs

and his back; he went into the hospital for five days of intensive treatment with some new, stronger chemotherapy. His hair fell out. Mom gave me the reports, saying Bob had asked that I not phone him, he "doesn't want to talk about it."

Suddenly I saw myself as he must have seen me, as I really was. I'd had a brother all my life and wasted him. Did I deserve to call him brother?

Bob was due to be a grandfather in three months. We all prayed he would live to see it. (Knock on wood.) If he could just hold out, he'd know that he'd lived a full life with all the major experiences. He kept fighting. His wife, that saint, kept him busy with engagements every night. Friends clustered around him.

Briefly, feeling that my life had already been fulfilled, I entertained the conceit that I would trade him my life if I could. But I had no choice in the matter, so this life-giving was just an exercise. I couldn't even give him my blood, it was the wrong type.

After the last course of chemo, the last round of radiation, there was another shadow on his lung. The tumors had returned. *Then I'm a dead man!* he cried aloud. Into the phone he cried, *Alix, I'm a dead man!*

I flew to his funeral from Italy, in the middle of my honeymoon. Twenty-four hours in transit, outfitted in new black Italian shoes and dress—as if even at his funeral I wanted to upstage him. Not until I stood in the chapel beside our grieving parents to recite the Kaddish together did I see that though I had not caused the burdens of his life, which began before I was born, I had never done anything—not one thing—to ease them. We'd remained rivals to the end. Now, in a triumph soured by grief, I emerged the winner, the one who survives to tell the tale.

....

Rereading Bob's obituary, folded neatly among his letters and souvenirs in the middle drawer of the bureau in the middle room, it suddenly struck me for the first time: he too was like our parents. Not as I was, but in his own way. His prudence, calculation, frugality, his playing by the rules were like Dad's. His community service, strong opinions, and earnestness, like Mom's. Only after his children finished college and moved to Chicago did he buy his town house—*like Mom,* I thought, moving to Shaker as soon as her children left home. And when he learned he had cancer, he vowed: I'm going to beat this thing like Mom did.

Over the years we'd each claimed alliance with our parents, each believing we alone understood them, thinking to take their side against the other—as if they were not equally ours. Still, Bob was often angry at them, disapproved of their opinions, badgered them about decisions, condemned Mom's assertiveness, and tried, Mom said, to bully them. After one of his campaigns to get Mom and Dad to trade their Shaker house for an apartment to be more age-appropriate, save money, and live more easefully, which Mom considered the first step on the road to putting them in a nursing home, she wrote a codicil to her will disinheriting anyone who put her in a home without the written agreement of all four grandchildren. Because I'd taken her side, he considered the codicil a personal affront, which he never forgave. Likewise, after she sold a Dubuffet sculpture to provide Bob with funds for alternative cancer therapies not covered by health insurance, he was furious to discover that another codicil provided an equal sum to me.

Their fetish for equality, originally intended to benefit him, he read as favoring me. He saw our parents every week, attended to their needs, watched over them, while I breezed into town maybe once a year. Why, he asked, shouldn't he inherit more than I? How unjust that I could claim my birthright by merely showing up now and then—like the Rockefellers closing off Rockefeller Center one day each year to preserve their title. He was the firstborn, the devoted son, he deserved the birthright.

It's an ancient story, going back to Genesis, which tells how Jacob, younger brother to the firstborn Esau, tricked their father out of Esau's rightful blessing. Learning of it, Esau "cried out with an exceedingly great and bitter cry, and said to his father, 'Bless me, even me also, O my father! . . . [Jacob] took away my birthright; and behold, now he has taken away my blessing.' . . . And Esau lifted up his voice, and wept. . . . Now Esau hated Jacob because of the blessing with which his father blessed him." Nevertheless, Jacob prevailed.

On Bob's last visit to New York and his first to my loft (which he circled with fascination, saying, So this is what they mean by a loft—I see—a whole apartment in one big room), he told me proudly that he had bought himself a Cadillac. Because, he explained, I've always wanted to drive a Cadillac. I was surprised, now that his days were numbered, and given his frugality—holding the purse strings of his family as tightly as our father had ours, always bugging our parents to sell their house. Why not buy it if that's what I want? he said. I can afford it, so why the hell not buy it? For our father, being able to afford something was never a reason to buy it. But for our mother it was reason enough. Again I was struck by the thought, He's like our mother, who wanted not a Cadillac but a large house, fine china, a mink coat, an art collection.

From the start I had defined myself in my difference from our family—first from Bob, then from Mom and from

Dad—playing each off against the other in the inner drama of my life. Had I not magnified our differences I might never have been able to leave. All at once I understood that though the balance of our parents' traits in each of us might vary and shift, like sunlight and shade through a screen door, the life-giving source was the same. Which meant we could each possess them both. Because in the end, to have them meant simply to love them. Sadly, I didn't understand this till Bob was dead. Perhaps if I had learned it sooner, we might have had each other too.

*

Squirreled away in Mom's files and Dad's dresser were the two halves of a correspondence between them from September 1931, when Mom went to Pennsylvania to help care for the newborn Bob, his sister Marian, and their grieving father, Louis. A decade after women won the vote, in a marriage of profound mutual respect and proclaimed equality, the separate spheres that ruled my parents' marriage from beginning to end stand revealed in every letter, alongside their affection and desires.

Each addresses the other, "Dearest Bummer" (Mom's spelling) or "Dearest Bumber" (Dad's). In Mom's first letter she requests that Dad please phone a certain Dr. Grossman about the baby's jaundice, bloodstained urine, Similac formula, and facial rash. Then she urges Dad to write her everything he's doing and thinking.

The next day, after beginning abruptly, "Why haven't you written to me?" Dad reports on his work, complaining about a judge whose "asinine remarks throughout the trial made it hard for me to keep a straight face," and on the domestic front: "I have canceled our milk order so that I may have sweet and not sour milk." "Be a good girl," he ends, "and don't forget to love your . . . Bumber."

In the next pair of letters the sentiment heats up. Mom's begins, "Dearest Sammie: I love you so much," while the following day Dad's begins, "Dearest Dorothy, Bumber, Darling, Sweetheart, Angel, Bonnie-girl, Kewpie, Mona Lisa, Dawthy-girl." He reports from Dr. Grossman that "the orange-color of Bobbie's urine is from the jaundice; Similac may be used if the baby thrives on it; use cornstarch for the rash." He then confesses, "When I read your letter I got a real thrill—and felt quite empty and 'funny.' "

Mom's letter is full of domestic instruction about laundry, housecleaning, clothes closets, dust. "We must prevent moths and bugs from getting a foot-hold," she warns, immediately adding a compensatory, "You know, I love you, dear." She advises Dad to dispose of spoiling food in "the breadbox, icebox, fruit bowl, or shelves," and to reduce the milk order—unaware that Speedy Sam has already canceled it on his own. Finally she asks Dad please to notify her professor "that my sister-in-law died leaving two orphans, one six days old. That I am keeping house for my brother for a few weeks until more permanent and satisfactory arrangements can be worked out. That I wish to continue our project upon my return"—adding, "I ask all this because I love you."

In her next letter she rejoices: "I just got your second letter a few minutes ago. So far I have read it three times." The baby, she reports, "is much improved and gets more adorable every day," and after requesting that when he comes down for the weekend Dad bring with him from Uncle Abe's drugstore some cod liver oil, antiseptic for mosquito bites, and "a box of cleenex [sic] towels" she asks, "How did Dr. Grossman say to use the cornstarch?"

Perversely writing about money on "Yom Kippur Day, 1931," freethinking Dad begins his next letter: "Darling

Bumber, You today became the owner of twenty, and I of thirty, shares of Republic Steel Corporation common stock, which I hope will be worth (your twenty, I mean) $1,000.00 in three or four years. The cost for all 50 was $325.00. This will be the last of our investments for a while, at least. . . . While at the broker's, I heard one of the men say that a Pittsburgh bank with $50,000,000 of deposits had failed. I thought at first it might be the one where your brother Harry banks, but heaved a sigh of relief to find that their money is in the Mellon bank, which is the best of them all." Then Dad cautions, in quotation marks, " 'We must economize, darling.' " After pages of family news ("Eddie picked up Mother and Pops in Shool today. He walked in hatless and got away again before anyone had a chance to throw him out. Pops was terribly embarrassed"), he ends, "I hope this letter is gossipy enough to suit you."

Having himself purchased two copies of Richman's *Laughs from Jewish Lore* "for our respective mothers," Dad bugs Mom to send: a housewarming present for H.R., a note to his sister Sophie, and a card to his sister Mame for her twentieth birthday. Then: "Will you 'receive' me cordially, enthusiastically, and lovingly, when I come next *Saturday evening*? . . . Baby bumber—I feel awful empty without you—and can't sleep very well because even in my sleep I miss you—I want you, sweetheart—I want you, bumber—I want you, darling—I want you, angel—I want you. I want you."

And there is Mom, after her endearments ("Bummer dear, it seems so strange to me now that in all the time you were here . . . I did not get a chance to tell you just how much I love you and have missed you"), urging him once again to have the house cleaned, the furniture brushed, and the closets sprayed because "I am worried about my fall coat in the clothes closet." Practical matters disposed of, she gets to the crux:

> Now that I have held Bobbie a few times, given him his bottle, and taken a little care of him, I think he is an adorable, helpless little bundle of sweetness. . . . In all seriousness, what is your feeling about taking Bobbie for a year? If we should decide to take him I might consider having one of my own now, if ever.

(How strange to see myself wedged between a *now* and an *if ever,* helped into being by my brother Bob!) To which Dad, clearing his throat and squaring his shoulders on the page, responds:

> To speak honestly, Honey-girl, I have my doubts as to whether you'd be very happy taking care of a baby not your own for a whole year, with the prospect of losing another year of the kind of activity you're so fond of when and if you should have one of your own. Personally, I'm highly in favor of the nursery alternative, for your sake, my sake and the baby's sake, but I shall be very happy to cooperate to the very fullest extent if you really wish and decided to take the youngster. Please consider this matter very fully and do not make any *impulsive* decisions which may possibly be regretted at a later date. The burden and responsibility will of course be mainly yours, and you are the one to decide. I shall be quite willing to abide by your decision. The thought is quite noble—but are you ready for canonization?

It was Mom's will, with Dad's sufferance, that prevailed in this as in so many matters. Without his encouragement, and alone of all her siblings, she checked the box "Nuclear Family" and played it out to the end. Was she the author of her own desires? If not she, certainly not Dad. "You are the one to decide," he told her, and "I shall abide by your decision." I know of nothing important she wanted that he ever actually vetoed. Though she may often have reined in her yearnings in deference to his, if he didn't oblige her she usually found a way. She got her children, her house, her travels, her art. And hers was the spelling of Bummer they ultimately adopted though Dad was known as the crack speller.

*

After Bob was buried, I went alone to my seaside cabin on the island in Maine to write and stayed there for five months. In the October woods the leaves had turned and begun to fall. My nearest neighbors had gone back to Canada for the winter, leaving me the last resident on the beach. I was trudging up the dirt road on my way to the mailbox at the top of the hill when I observed the thick piles of leaves—oak, maple, birch, and shrub—lining the road. Because I was alone and free, I abandoned the clean center crown to crunch and crackle along the edge of the road. Stomping my way up the hill, jumping up and down on the piled-up leaves to make all the noise I could, I suddenly remembered how as children my brother and I had delighted to rake the leaves into giant heaps, then leap on top of them, rescattering them, and rake them again for our father to burn. A major autumn joy. It never occurred to us to grieve for the leaves; we never thought of them as dead or dying. Autumn was as new and dazzling and throbbing with life to us as spring, the deep snows of winter to follow as welcome as summer sizzle.

I collected my mail, mostly junk, and crunching back

down the hill with my eyes to the ground I bent down to re-
trieve a particularly huge oak leaf, then a brilliant red
maple that caught my eye, then a sprig of dried tiny daisy-
like flowers I can't name, and one raspberry leaf peculiarly
edged in greenish-white where the underside had begun to
curl in. I remembered leaves traced on unlined three-ring
paper, traced like our kindergarten hands, pasted to windows, identified, leaves of trees Bob and I pressed between
leaves of books. Not since then had I collected autumn
leaves for the fun of it. On the beach, wind whipped my
poncho around my calves, pulled off my hood; I protected
my treasures in a large mailer from some ambitious investment firm, which I recognized as just like the mailer my
brother's insurance company yearly used for sending out
the calendar printed with his name followed by "Million
Dollar Round Table."

After that, every time I climbed the hill for the mail and
heard the crackling of the leaves, I thought of Bob with sor-
row and remorse. Every leaf I picked up sent me back to
him, my brother, my crunching mate, who arrived to our
parents just long enough before me to ensure that he would
always be bigger, but not so much bigger that I couldn't aspire to pass him. My brother, who in autumn sometimes
permitted me to play touch football with him and his
friends or lent me his knife though never his marble
shooter, who famously shielded me from a certain dog and
shared his wagon when we canvassed our neighborhood
for toothpaste tubes, flattened tin cans, and bundled news-
papers to help fight the war though our classes were com-
petitors. I suddenly saw how in all things he was my
original, my primal, competitor. It was against him that I
learned to measure, wrestle, outwit, unscruple, and win.
Against him I learned to turn my handicaps—my age, size,

sex—to advantage and perfidy. Ah, my brother, how easily I unmanned you once I learned the knack, how meanly I bested you and then savored each sweet victory, each guilty satisfaction. And even after we parted company, how stubbornly I held onto the birthright.

Now I wonder if Bob didn't outdo me after all. For a year before my birth and for two years before his death, he was the focus of our mother's every thought. (Only now, when they are mine alone, do I call them our mother and our father; while Bob lived they were simply Mom and Dad or, secretly, my mother, my father.) When he died, she too began to die, as if her one desire were to join him. He never had to witness her decline or put her in the dreaded nursing home. And through his enigmatic silence he has made me write this book.

Chapter 14

After Bob's children and I had taken what we wanted from the house, my job was to get the best possible prices for all that remained. The furnishings would be easy: even a small classified notice of a liquidation sale on Shaker Boulevard brought dealers and buyers lining up in their cars outside the house at dawn. In one swoop everything would disappear—all those elegant 7AAA high-heeled pumps, the embroidered table linens, the music of a lifetime. I interviewed three liquidators and selected one.

Determined to solve the mystery of the padlocked bottom drawer in Dad's closet before the liquidators took over, I collected all the keys scattered through the house and tried each one until at last the lock yielded its secret. Pulling open the drawer, I was disappointed to find it filled not, as I had fantasized, with love letters or scandalous photos or golden coins or stock certificates. Instead there were several dozen tiny glass bottles of assorted booze—cognac, scotch, bourbon, liqueurs—the kind that long ago were given out free on airplanes. Oh, my teetotaling frugal father! I packed the bottles among my clothes to take back to New York to offer to my friends.

Disposing of the art I knew would be trickier. Knowledge of the market was crucial, and I was ignorant.

Years before, Mom had advised sending her collection to one of the large New York auction houses, Sotheby's or Christie's, should it ever come to that. Though out of my depth, dutifully I arranged for Sotheby's and Christie's to appraise the works. Then a local auctioneer-dealer named Martin Fox came to appraise the antiques. As soon as he took off his coat, he glanced to the far wall of the living room and his mouth dropped.

"Don't tell me you've got a de Kooning here."

I nodded.

"What's it doing here?"

"My mother's a collector."

He whistled a low wolf whistle. I saw the numbers clicking behind his eyes as he took in the collection, so unexpected here in Cleveland, watched his excitement mount as he moved down the room from the steel Caro sculpture at one end to the Stella collage over the mantle, the Olitski oil beside the fireplace, the Nevelson construction over the chess table, the Motherwell collage above the ancient Magnavox, and the brilliant Frankenthaler canvas beside it. As he pressed on to the dining room where among a half-dozen paintings and drawings he spotted Avery's landscape hanging over the sideboard, agitation spilled from him like musk.

He turned to me, all charm. "Are you, uh, planning to sell the art too?"

"Some of it," I said.

"You're going to keep the de Kooning, of course."

"I don't think so. Maybe the Nevelson."

"And the rest?" he asked hungrily. "What do you plan to do with it?"

"I'll probably send it to New York for auction."

It was as if I'd struck him with a club. "Oh, noooooo," he moaned, grabbing his head. "You don't want to do that . . ."

And from that moment on, for the next several months, he pursued a relentless seductive campaign to get me to consign the works to him.

What should I do? I knew nothing about the art world. Adopting my father's puritanical posture, I'd always held myself aloof from Mom's collecting—though over the years Dad himself, impressed by Mom's business acumen, had become her champion. Whenever I'd visited Cleveland, no sooner had I deposited my bag upstairs and changed my clothes than he whisked me off to see her latest addition. Then a fast tour of the collection, with Dad exuding equal parts incredulity and admiration as he recited the names of the eminent artists whose work graced their walls, hoping I might share in Mom's delight as he had learned to do. But, suspecting Mom of base motives, I remained detached, as if there were room in our family for but a single legitimate ambition: my own.

"Do whatever you think best," Dad said now. Having made me trustee of their estates, he refused even to venture an opinion.

Had she been capable of an opinion, Mom would have known precisely what to do. She'd been collecting art since her twenties, when she and her sister Celia, each newly married, began adorning their walls with signed and numbered etchings, engravings, lithographs, and woodcuts that they ordered from the catalogues of the Associated American Artists in New York or from the Print Club of Cleveland. The halls of my youth were decked with images: an odalisque by Matisse with circles for breasts and oval for face; a puzzling Rockwell Kent of a man carrying a rock that looked to me like his own knee; the differing dragons of Dali (pierced by a mounted St. George) and Frasconi (a crocodile stalking a dog); the anonymous etching of a young girl with exposed backside that Dad found objectionable. There were the angular houses of Lyonel Feininger, the female Buddhas of Shiko Munakata, the chugging locomotives of Reginald Marsh, the tortuous clouds of Thomas Hart Benton. Soon there were too many pictures for the walls, and Mom began rotating the exhibits.

Then in 1967, the same year I discovered feminism, she boosted her collecting to an entirely new plane. With her children gone and her writing long abandoned, she began to create herself anew through art. Borrowing against her insurance policies for the first down payment, she took a risky leap, buying on time the founding piece of her collection, an abstract 22-by-30-inch watercolor landscape in blues, purples, and greens, of stylized clouds, tree, mountain, and ground by the American painter Milton Avery, entitled *Purple Mountain Landscape*. The total price was $1,600—more than the value of all her prints combined. The framed color reproduction of a Cézanne landscape that had hung over the mantel was relegated to an upstairs hall and the Avery installed in its place of honor.

After that, through concentrated study and savvy trading up she built her collection. Starting on borrowed funds, she was as resourceful as a mogul, gaining financial leverage by conserving her household allowance and learning the legal loopholes whereby she could donate art to museums for tax deductions, which she traded to Dad at tax time for cash that she promptly reinvested in downpayments on more art. To make room for the large new acquisitions, gradually she moved the prints to upstairs walls or gave them to Bob. She plunged into Cleveland's small contemporary art world, once again merging her private and public passions. All through the 1970s and 1980s she embraced and championed local artists, organizing exhibitions of their works at the gallery she now ran for the Women's City Club, and writing up interviews with them for a new bimonthly art journal. Enthusiastically she bought their works to hang on her walls alongside the international stars.

Would she, so shrewd in the business of art, find it as difficult as I to resist the seductive blandishments of super-salesman Martin Fox? The deal he dangled before me grew steadily sweeter as we dickered: Control over the reserve (minimum) prices of each work up until the final gavel. A mere token sales commission, a fraction of New York rates. A waiver of all the standard charges and penalties. A guaranteed blitz of pre-auction publicity. And, finally, a full-color catalogue picturing the de Kooning on the cover, to include Mom's entire collection down to the least significant print, and to feature a portrait of Mom and a biographical sketch of her as a collector, which I could write myself. Compared to Sotheby's, whose appraiser was willing to take only the collection's most "important" pieces (excluding the pseudo-Prendergast and local works) and under a contract involving low reserve prices and hefty charges for everything from crating, shipping, and insurance to outrageous penalties should the works fail to bring their minimums, Fox's deal began to look irresistible—especially when I imagined the pleasure the catalogue would give my parents.

I consulted Mom's colleagues: fellow collectors, dealers, even the Cleveland Museum's curator of contemporary art. Their advice on where to sell was equivocal: while they assured me that Fox was reputable and his auction house one of the best in the region, the regional pool of bidders would be small.

So here it was again—the old question of fish size relative to pond size, of Cleveland versus New York. For myself that choice had been a snap, and once made never reconsidered. So heedlessly had I rejected everything about my native city that I once arrogantly planned to write a book exposing the bourgeois provincialism of Cleveland's eastern suburbs—my "Cleveland book," I called it—as if it were simply the place I'd fled rather than the place my people lived. The final chapter was to be called "Cleveland Collects Art"—after a Cleveland Museum of Art exhibition of works of contemporary art lent by Cleveland collectors, in which three of Mom's pieces were (anonymously) shown. Lucky for me, my editor killed that book, returning my proposal with the disparaging question, How many people do you think really want to read about Cleveland?—saving me from mocking in print my mother's chief passion without a thought of the betrayal. So thoughtless was I on the subject that once, as I was starting to lay into the place, Dad, sensing the coming assault, pushed back my words with an upheld palm and said, Now don't you go bashing Cleveland. That was my first inkling that he took my aspersions personally. By that time the city that had once been a place of booming ethnic variety and industry—a world complete—had become the butt of a national joke. A comedian had only to pronounce the name Cleveland to get a laugh. I wasn't sure exactly why—though I laughed too. The dead lake on its shore? The infamous river so polluted it caught on fire and inspired a song? My father, offended, did not laugh.

Now, representing not myself but my mother, my personal rejection of Cleveland was irrelevant. Confronted by the experts' obvious respect for Mom as a serious collector, I had to abandon the smug disdain I'd harbored for so many years thinking, this is Cleveland, not life—as if Mom's knowledge, passion, and joy in art were merely expressions of provincial vanity.

I began to suspect that it was less Mom's vanity that Fox's catalogue would feed than my own need to redeem myself. She had never been vain about collecting. Glad, tickled, even proud, but hardly vain. When she lent or donated her pieces, it was usually anonymously; her life with art brought her more pleasure than pride. In any case, she had lost her capacity to read, which meant that the catalogue, however lavish, would be wasted on her.

Not, however, on me. It was chastening to realize that in order to write the brief profile of Mom for Fox's catalogue I'd have to study the documentary record pieced together from her files, just like any stranger.

Indeed, some strangers were more familiar with her work than I was. I knew the bare outlines, having read the one-page summaries of their lives Speedy Sam had prepared for obituary time. But until recently I had avoided thinking much about her activities, dismissing them as the projects of the privileged—as though I weren't myself a lucky product of that privilege. But now when people stopped by our table in Fisher Dining Room to pay homage to Mom, I had to take note. Here was a woman whose daughter Mom had helped get a scholarship to the Cleveland Institute of Music. Here was someone who had worked with Mom on the Kennedy campaign. And one evening, just as I was getting ready to unfold my parents' aluminum walkers and lead them back to their rooms, we were delayed by a woman in a wheelchair who rolled herself up to our table and said: "You probably don't remember me, Dorothy, but I remember you well. Back when we worked together, I thought you were the smartest, sharpest gal in the whole city. I think I was in awe of you. Nothing could stop you. You were always out there, giving them what-for." Then, opening wide her sunken eyes and shaking her bony head, she pronounced, "You were some cookie, lady!"

Puzzled, Mom whispered to me incredulously, "I was a cookie lady?"

The tributes may have been lost on Mom, but they were finally getting through to me.

*

As I sat beside my mother turning pages of the catalogue in which her entire art collection was pictured, she seemed genuinely pleased. Had she accepted the sale as inevitable, or did she fail to comprehend the implications?

Her comprehension had grown increasingly erratic. That very afternoon she had asked my husband and me if we were married.

"Mom, you were at our wedding," I said. "You did your Marlene Dietrich imitation of 'Falling in Love Again.' You wore that wonderful grey silk suit."

She thought a moment, then said, "I don't remember the suit, but I'm glad I looked nice. The song, though, I do remember." And dropping her voice into her lowest register and tilting her head at a rakish angle, she sang again, with all the old charm, Dietrich's signature song.

Afterward she said cheerfully, without a trace of irony, "It's nice to recall those memories, don't you think? What is life, after all, if not our memories?"

My husband and I exchanged a look. Could she be completely oblivious of her condition?

A moment later she again inquired if we were married. I was surprised that she'd forgotten our wedding since we'd married partly for her. For ourselves, having lived together contentedly for years we'd felt no particular need to marry. But when my brother began to die, tearing the family apart, I thought that our marriage might somehow comfort Mom and Dad. The urge to separate my life from theirs even to the point of excluding them from my previous wedding had finally dissipated when my brother was dying. Planning our wedding, I imagined a small family ceremony with all of us together one last time. But in the end Bob was too weak to attend.

"Yes, Mom," I repeated, "you were at our wedding."

"Really! I was?" Then she added with that easy laugh I always loved, "I don't remember that."

This time it was my turn to tell her reassuringly, as she had once told me, "You don't have to remember. It's enough that it's true."

*

The auction, to which I flew weeks after the liquidation sale, was held at Fox's on a Saturday in late summer. Neither of my parents attended; Mom couldn't and Dad declined.

The spacious downtown hall, hung to the ceiling with art and *objets,* was packed with people. There had been a flurry of publicity hyping the auction, including mass mailings to dealers in major cities and well-illustrated news stories in the Cleveland papers, both daily and Sunday. "While many of Dorothy Davis Kates' neighbors were surely decorating their Shaker Heights homes with an eye toward matching still lifes with sofas, Kates was gathering works by Frank Stella, Willem de Kooning and Helen Frankenthaler," read the lead sentence of the Arts & Living section. Quoting the curator of contemporary art at the Cleveland Museum, the article went on to praise Mom as " 'an energetic and passionate collector who did her homework.' "

On a platform at the front of the room, half a dozen aides manned a bank of phones to handle telephone bids, while nearby four burly men stood like bodyguards or bouncers ready to move the pieces quickly on and off the stage at a signal from the auctioneer. Martin Fox circulated nervously.

I sat near the back with my husband, holding a numbered bidding paddle, hoping to avoid recognition. I needn't have worried; except for the few people who quietly greeted me with what seemed a funerary air while the crowd was assembling, as if to acknowledge the end of an era, everyone was a stranger. Evidently my parents had outlived most of their friends and whatever enemies might otherwise have come to gape or gloat.

This was only the third auction I'd ever attended, my first as a seller. A few months earlier, to prepare myself, I'd sat through Sotheby's New York auction of contemporary art; but then, as now, it all went by so fast and so quietly that I could barely follow it. By the time the Fox auctioneer reached the Kates Collection—the climax of the auction—I was still unsure of the fine points of procedure and could not always understand the bidding. How I wished my mother could be there to guide me.

Most of the small pieces and prints sold easily, but several of the major ones failed to bring their minimums, which meant that they would have to be sold in New York after all. Like my adaptable parents, I thought this the best of both worlds: the catalogue and hoopla in Cleveland, plus the savvy of a New York dealer. With any luck, between the proceeds of the house and the art there would be no shortage of money to cover whatever level of care my parents might require in their remaining time at Judson and on earth. Mom, in diapers and unable to find her way to the dining room on her own but still able to feed herself, was already at the second-highest care level. I feared that Dad, with his failing heart and his proclivity to fall, might be joining her any day. Naturally, the greater the care, the higher the cost. But also, I realized, as I sat with my parents in Dad's apartment after the auction enjoying the last flowering of Judson's late summer garden, even at an award-winning, nonprofit institution like Judson Park, the greater the care, the smaller the room.

iv | *Midair*

. . . as if an airplane had stopped midair . . .

— SIMONE DE BEAUVOIR, *A Very Easy Death*

Judson's Casino Party, January 1, 1996.
Dad, 94, and Mom, 88, celebrate their final
New Year.

Chapter 15

My parents had rushed to my rescue whenever I needed rescuing. Now I'd had the unexpected opportunity of returning the favor. But sometimes it came over me that I had perhaps done the opposite, that by moving them from their house to Judson—a move for which they'd once stood ready to disinherit Bob—I had let them down again, despite my daily phone calls and attentions.

Which version was true? How could I tell?

Reading the gratitude and pride in Daddy's eyes as he stroked my hand in his cozy apartment, I could bask in requital. Surrounded by the familiar furniture I'd moved from the Shaker house, with his important papers filed in his desk, Dad seemed content. But when my mother, nodding in a chair in her fifth-floor room in Breuning, looked up with astonished joy to see me coming through the door (whether following an absence of a single night or a month) and clapped her hands and cried in an ecstasy of relief like a sprung prisoner, "Oh, my darling Alix! You're here!" my heart contracted with guilt.

Not that I hadn't done my best for her. I had seen that her nurses were kind; I'd installed a radio tuned to the classical music station; I'd supplemented the institutional fluorescent light with two exquisite porcelain lamps that had sat on her bedroom dresser, and hung on her walls bright works of contemporary art and that signed picture of Bill and Hillary Clinton. I bought knee-hi's to replace the panty hose, now so difficult to yank up over her diapers, and replaced her silk blouses and woolen skirts with sturdy new clothes that could survive the institutional washing machines and dryers. Yet despite her obvious pleasure as we gossiped and reminisced during my sporadic visits, left to herself she sat staring into space, rising only to push her walker to the bathroom, grunting "Ooh, ooh, ooh, ooh." Once I heard her ask in a whisper, "Suppose we wanted to leave here, Sam, could we?" and I'd rushed to answer, "But Mom, where would you go?" After that, I was often stricken by the question, blinding as an interrogator's beam: *Was* she a prisoner? And a prisoner of what?

It was the rapid deterioration of both my parents within months of their move to Judson—Dad's hospitalization for heart failure, Mom's move to the dementia ward—that made me unsure if I had rescued or condemned them. Perhaps it would have happened anywhere: no one lives forever. But our family was spoiled: Grandma Davis had lived to a hundred, Grandpa Davis to eighty-nine, Grandma Kates to eighty-seven, Aunt Lil and Aunt Eva into their nineties—and Dad himself didn't even retire fully till ninety. On each birthday my parents speculated about whether or not they would "make it" to a hundred, as if that were the undisputed goal, and death was for other families.

As always, they adapted to each new crisis with its subsequent slip toward dependency: the falls that put them each on walkers, then in wheelchairs; the increasing incontinence that brought the indignity of diapers. How volubly they loved me then! Mom seemed to become more affectionate with each regression. Was it her nature ripening or her need? I had always felt cherished by my parents, but now she treated me, and Dad too, like saviors. Her stories were undamaged: she could reminisce for hours, reiterating her shrewd pronouncements on the past. Yet she was unable to make the simplest decision in her present life. So complete was her disorientation that she could no longer find the way to her bathroom, though it was only steps from her chair. "Now what should I do?" she asked when, feeling the urge, she rose to her feet.

"Just keep going straight ahead, Mom, take another step, that's it"—until she asked again, "Tell me what to do next." Sometimes I wondered if her incontinence was merely an inability to find the bathroom.

When Dad had kidnapped Mom, I'd counted among the rewards her being able to dine again in the elegant Fisher Dining Room—so much more suitable, I thought, for the woman who was said to have set the most exquisite table in all of Cleveland than the shocking fifth-floor dining room, with its plastic table pads, terrycloth bibs, set meals, and unearthly screams. But after three weeks Mom was barred from Fisher because she kept throwing her diapers down the toilet or leaving them on the floor of the women's room, which Dad could not enter to assist her. After that, she was permitted in Fisher only when I came to town and could take her to the bathroom. Appalled by the alternating silence and ruckus on five, I thought that eating in Fisher with me and Dad would give her as much pleasure as it gave me. Hadn't she herself been embarrassed to the point of apology by the strange outbursts of some of the fifth-floor residents? But as time went on, she grew accustomed to the disruptive sounds—or perhaps she no longer noticed them. Soon Dad was joining her for lunch, then for dinner too. They both seemed satisfied. After my first meal with them on five, I had to admit that after all, having to choose from a menu only confused her, and now they both did better with a bib.

It was in the fifth-floor dining room halfway to Mom's table that my father died. Or so it seemed at first. He collapsed to the floor from cardiac arrest. No nurse could find a pulse or breath. Then after two full minutes, as suddenly as he fell, he sat straight up with his back erect and his twigs of legs stretched out in front of him, gasping for breath.

On my New York answering machine I found a message with the news that he'd been rushed to the hospital. I was frantic at the phrase *cardiac arrest*. Part of me had been expecting his demise every day. I knew his heart was shot. But when I heard those words, I began to fall apart. It was irrational: at ninety-four, with all his mental faculties still intact, Dad had probably lived long enough. I astonished myself with my uncontrollable grief.

Frantically I telephoned Judson. "He may be all right. It was a completely spontaneous recovery," said the nurse, whose orders were DNR: Do Not Resuscitate.

Mom and Dad had been regularly showering their children and grandchildren with DNR orders and living wills since 1969, when Grandma Davis, hospitalized shortly before her one hundredth birthday, had been kept wretchedly alive through forced feeding. Mom described the ordeal in her first published essay, "The Facts of Death."

> ... A stomach tube was inserted through Mother's nose. Several times a day, nurses arrived with strained foods which were poured directly through the tube. Mother found the whole procedure miserably uncom-

fortable. . . . In the beginning, she still had enough strength to jerk the tube out. The nurses would replace it. When left alone, Mother would remove it. Her physician, not to be deterred from his course, ordered her arms tied to the bed.

Now began her time of agony. She begged me, she begged the doctor, she begged the nurses, she begged everyone who came into her room to untie her hands. She pleaded; she explained that now she was unable to turn over, unable to use a handkerchief, unable even to scratch an itch. Her blind eye had tended for years to tear excessively. She could not dry her tears.

The days stretched into weeks. There was no relief from the stomach tube nor the tied hands. Her every waking moment was spent in pleading with everyone who came into her room to release her.

I could not bear her misery. I discussed the situation repeatedly with the physician. How long did he plan to continue this treatment? "Oh, permanently," he said, explaining to me that her faculties were so far impaired that she could not remember not to pull out the tube.

With the tube still down her nose and her hands tied to her bed, three days after her one hundredth birthday Grandma Davis finally escaped through the mercy of death, becoming both a legend and a caution to the family: DNR: Do Not Resuscitate.

In the hospital a pacemaker was installed in Dad's heart to forestall further blackout falls. When I inquired after Mom, who had witnessed Dad's fall and was again bewildered and alone, the nurse on the phone passed my question to Mom's aide. "How's Mrs. Kates reacting to Mr.

Kates being gone?" she asked. I heard the aide's faint answer through the phone: " 'Ooh, ooh, ooh.' "

Upon release from the hospital Dad returned not to his apartment but to a Nursing room on six for rehabilitation. He needed it: the hospital procedure and his new medications had finally reduced him to dependence. Massive doses of Lasix, the diuretic, rendered him incontinent; the drug to regulate his pacemaker blurred his mind, speech, and orientation; his glasses never made it back from the hospital; and concern about his falling landed him in a wheelchair with a buzzer on his leg set to go off whenever he tried to stand unassisted. Then after a month of rehabilitation he was judged no longer fit for Independent Living, or even Assisted Living.

I disagreed. True, he was weak and for a while he continued to fall, but he kept coming back, responding with his customary acceptance and dignity. He removed the buzzer whenever he went to the bathroom and when he rolled his wheelchair through the halls to visit Mom. One night he made his way all the way down to Security for a spare key to his old apartment, to which he repaired for the night. Discovering him missing from his bed, his aide and a nurse began a search that ended in his apartment, where they found him in the marital bed asleep, with his clothes folded neatly on a chair. They promptly woke him and took him back to Nursing.

As soon as his drug dosages were adjusted, his mind came back. During my next visit he dictated to me three thank-you letters with his usual aplomb. Though he had stopped reading books, with the replacement trifocals I procured for him he read the newspaper every morning at breakfast and the Ohio Bar reports that arrived regularly in the mail. He was not permitted to keep cash in his Nursing room, but he refused to get a haircut without having a tip to give the barber. To solve the problem he asked me to mail him a check for $20, which he took to the bank and cashed en route to the barbershop. Scrupulously he maintained his standards.

On the other hand, he disregarded the exposé of the Million Dollar Lottery I had clipped from the *New York Times* and mailed to him and, still convinced that he was about to win, resubscribed to *Time*. He often smelled of urine, no longer bothered to insert his hearing aid, could barely keep the bridge attached to his gums, and sometimes fell. Despite his graduation back from confusion to clarity and from wheelchair to walker, a final staff conference judged him in need of permanent nursing care.

When a room became available, he was moved from the rehabilitation section on six to a regular Nursing room on four, with a shared bathroom. I flew to Cleveland for a long weekend to empty the apartment and get him settled into his newly reduced quarters. As once again I emptied drawers, closets, cupboards, culling the indispensable records and precious papers preserved over generations to take back to New York, I sensed that each successive move had distilled my parents' lives like a long-simmered sauce reduced to essence.

After I'd moved into Dad's new room the few pieces of furniture that could reasonably fit, he looked around his bed and said, "This is a pretty small room." In a mere six months my parents had each gone from their six-bedroom Shaker palace to a single ten-by-ten-foot room, and were lucky to have it. "Would you like me to try to have you moved to a bigger room when one comes free?" I asked him. "Not really," he said. "I don't require much. I never have." Indeed, I believe that without Mom to spur them on he would have been content to spend his whole life in the rented side-by-side on Woodmere Road. He did not measure his life in real estate.

When I had the phone line transferred from the apartment to Dad's Nursing room, I discovered that I could order a phone for my mother's room as well. Mistakenly, I'd assumed that private phones were not permitted on the dementia ward. Now I rejoiced to be able to speak to her every day. Not that our conversations had much content, but they were reassuring to me and I hoped to her.

"How are you, Mom?" I would start.

"First-rate. How are you, dear?"

"I'm fine. What have you been doing today?"

"Not much. Resting my eyes."

"Did you have a nice lunch?"

If Dad was with her, she would say, "Did we have a nice lunch, Sam?" And if he wasn't there, she said, "Yes, I think so."

"What did you have?"

"Well, let me see now. . . . Bummer, what did we have for lunch?"

When we had said all that there was to say, I asked if I might speak to Dad.

"Yes, if I can find him."

"Is he there?"

"I think so."

"Then would you please hand him the phone?"

"I will if he's handy."

"Is he handy?"

"Let me see. Sam? Bummer?"

Sometimes Dad came on, but sometimes I waited quite a while before Mom finally reported, "He's not handy."

....

My conversations with both my parents grew more and more perfunctory. Their lives were so circumscribed that even Dad had little to report. When I tried to liven the exchange with questions about the past, his hearing often kept him from making out my words, though if I did manage to make myself understood, he answered me fully and precisely, down to the middle initial of each of his office colleagues on the tenth floor of the Hippodrome Building back in the 1940s. And sometimes he astonished me with feats of hearing, as when he told me that his new suite mate had a daughter who was "quite a philosopher."

"How do you know that?" I asked.

"I hear them talking."

"You mean you listen?"

"When she's there, yes," he said defiantly. "I enjoy listening to them."

But with his hearing aid permanently retired to a drawer, I wondered if he wasn't imagining as conversation our own past philosophical exchange. Among his papers I'd found a letter I had written him a decade earlier saying: "Each time I receive one of your beautifully constructed and gracefully written letters I remember anew how when I was a child you imbued me with the highest standards of language and thought, both by precept and example, and I thank you. You must not, I hope, take personally our unending imbroglios, except in the sense that you taught me how to argue and have always been and continue to be my best adversary. I delight in our heated discussions, even when they end in an impasse."

In other ways too he sometimes slipped into the past. His suite mate's wife told me that one day Dad walked into her husband's room and asked her to send birthday checks for

$5 each to his great-grandchildren, Lisa's boys—as if she were his trusted secretary, who kept his checkbook and would know exactly where to mail the checks.

With the house and apartment gone, when I visited them again in December I stayed in a Judson guestroom. It was just like their former apartment, only on a different floor. That visit took place on the weekend of the worst blizzard of the century. The airports were closed down for days and I had to stay much longer than planned. With my chores finished and no possibility of leaving the building, I had nothing to do but visit with my parents and observe. So it happened that I had meals in three different dining rooms, as if to recapitulate my parents' tenure at Judson: on Sunday, Dad and I went to the fancy Fisher Dining Room on six for Christmas dinner (held early since some of the residents would be gone for the actual holiday); on Monday, I lunched with him in his fourth-floor Nursing dining room; and at dinner that night he and I joined Mom on five in the dining room for dementia patients. I was amazed at the outcome.

In civilized Fisher we were seated at a table with another family: a resident, her son, and his wife. Aware that we were Jewish and inappropriately dressed—Dad's jacket was stained, I was wearing sneakers—I felt awkward at this formal Christian dinner. Our conversation, though polite, was painfully artificial and rife with the subtle self-promotion of society.

But at least we talked. The next day in Dad's dining room on four, where the patients suffered from physical rather than mental disorders, at our table there wasn't a word of conversation throughout lunch. All four residents were so focused on the difficult task of transporting their food to their mouths that they never looked up from their plates. I wondered if they were silent because of the hopelessness of their conditions or perhaps because, like my father, they had a hard time hearing. In that entire dining room the only conversation was among the aides who chatted with each other between the tables while they fed their wards.

At dinner that night in the dining room of the dementia ward, where Dad and I joined Mom, the conversation was warm and lively, despite its many impenetrable patches. The four elderly residents at our table—Mom, Sadie, Bertha, and Noreen—were considerate listeners and interesting talkers, though not always coherent. Each made allowances for the lapses and weirdnesses of the others, politely accepting one another's delusions. Noreen, a buxom, powdered redhead, told stories of her romantic triumphs as a Smith student at Ivy League football weekends as if they had just occurred, to which the others jumped in with sisterly advice. Petite, grandmotherly Bertha with the silver hair and glittering eyes was obsessed with World War I. Through the large window she searched the distant sky for rockets, cowering at every plane, and accepted the safe-airplane stories the rest of us offered her for comfort. Sadie's wry, exasperated commentary on the selfish outbursts occurring at other tables gave the conversation a certain unity and lightness. Everyone laughed, even Bertha, who clucked her tongue at Sadie's wicked scorn. Sadie's stream of low-keyed barbs delivered straight-faced and sotto voce out of the side of her thin mouth were so on-target and witty that I wondered why she was on the fifth floor at all until I saw her use her fork to open a tear in her bib, which she then spent twenty minutes picking apart thread by minute thread before she was able to eat. No one mentioned her odd behavior even though she was just getting started on her appetizer as the rest of us finished our main course. We so enjoyed ourselves that we lingered over dessert and were the last table to leave the dining room.

The next afternoon there was a Christmas singalong on Mom's floor. I got my parents into their wheelchairs and one at a time wheeled them down to the piano area. Christa, the recreational therapist and a fine soprano, sang into a mike while big Nancy accompanied her on the piano. I started to sing along but stopped when no one else joined in. When it was over, Mom and Dad, veteran concertgoers, applauded enthusiastically, but the rest of the group remained snoozing in their chairs as they had throughout. No one seemed to want to leave. Where would they go? To do what? I wondered as I wheeled my parents back to Mom's room.

By the time the snow stopped and the planes were again taking off, I was beginning to feel familiarly comfortable with the patients and their families, the staff and their routines. The residents' individual characters and personalities began to emerge as I recognized them in the halls and the dining rooms. Mostly they appeared to me much older and worse off than my parents. Yet I could see that to the aides and nurses, who saw them daily and laughed amiably at everyone, each resident was uniquely and equally strange. Sadie picked apart her bib, Noreen heard voices from the past, the flasher flashed, the screamer screamed, Dad puffed through the halls, and Mom said "Ooh, ooh, ooh, ooh" all the way home. My extra days with nothing much to do had enabled me to see that here was a daily life not unlike others, though slower and with less hope. Rise in the morning, toilet, eat, rest, another meal, then another, toilet, medication, to bed. With a flurry of activities in between, just like outside—only what there were considered extra chores to fit into a busy schedule here became the big events: a haircut, a trip to the bank, a doctor's visit, an exercise class. Since despite everything Mom seemed to me pretty much her old quirky self—no less affectionate or fun to be with than before, with most of her traits and memories intact—I had to concede that the same was probably true of the other residents. That whatever their disorders they remained to the end for better or worse themselves.

*

On my last visit to the dementia ward a new social worker on the floor with a European accent stopped me to say that recently she and Mom had been speaking French together. She was amazed at Mom's fluency and delight in the language, at Mom's easy use of all the expressions and idioms, at her memory for everything. She was even more amazed when I told her that Mom had not begun to study French till her fifties, and she scoffed at the suggestion that Mom had Alzheimer's. Indeed, said the social worker, Mom would do anything she was asked if the request were delivered in French. The previous day, for example, following a long bilingual chat, both my parents had for the first time joined an exercise group because the invitation had been issued in French. The social worker was so pleased that she planned to arrange regular French conversations with Mom.

Unfortunately, Mom died before they could get going. One night she had a stomachache; the next morning she returned from the bathroom to her bed and, like an airplane that had stopped midair, died.

Because she was my mother and eighty-nine, I'd assumed her life was endless. Confronted by the news, I suddenly saw that it was as fleeting as a gust of wind.

I flew at once to my father's side.

"She went so suddenly," said Dad, uncomprehending. "I didn't know she was that sick. She had a tummy ache for a day or two, but I had no idea she was going to die. . . . Afterward, I went up and saw her lying in bed. She looked as if she were asleep, her head to the side, her mouth open peacefully. . . . She certainly didn't look dead."

"You were a wonderful husband to her," I said.

"Not so wonderful."

"Of course you were, Daddy."

But he just shook his head sadly.

Six years before, in his memoir, he had written: "I believe myself to have been and still am a prompt, persistent, orderly, diligent, considerate, and generally kindly person. My wife charges me with being a nag; she also accuses me of having become crotchety in my old age. I deny the second charge."

Over lunch I asked my father what he thought was Mom's most outstanding quality. He cocked his head in concentration and said, "She was so full of life."

"What do you mean," I asked, "full of beans?"

Laughing, he said, "Indeed she was that. She was certainly full of beans." Then his face turned sober and he shook his head and repeated, "She didn't look dead at all."

As we rode the elevator back down to his room, an administrator with black hair and lots of makeup said with an animated smile, "Why, hello Mr. Kates. How are you today? And how is your wife?"

Dad looked at her for a moment as if she were crazy, then said almost angrily, "My wife? She's *dead*!"

The administrator took a step backward as if to avert a blow. "No!"

"Yes," I said, offering the consolation of truth, "she died this morning."

My consolation was to know that just before she died Mom had had a "nice long chat" in French. Perhaps that was why she looked so peaceful; perhaps she was looking forward to the next chat, her interest in life renewed. Yes, I decided, she died happily dreaming in French. What was the harm in thinking so?

Dad found a different comfort. A month after the funeral when I arrived at Judson for a visit, he said to me, "Say, Al, I haven't seen Dorothy in quite a while."

"I know, Daddy. She died."

"I don't think so," he said, tapping his spoon on his saucer.

I was shocked. He—the consummate skeptic, debunker of the afterlife, who wrote of his bar mitzvah, "That was the apogee of my religious beliefs; shortly thereafter I became a doubter."

"You don't? Then where do you think she is?"

"That I don't know. But I don't believe she's dead."

"Why not?"

"I saw her, and she didn't look dead. And . . . sometimes I hear her talking."

"She had a funeral," I offered.

"I know," he said. Still the skeptic, but with a difference—this time skeptical of death. Against such skepticism what weight could a mere funeral carry? Since Mom had been autopsied and cremated, in place of a casket a large candle with a flickering flame had represented her during the service. The rabbi, a commanding young woman in an embroidered yarmulke, gave an eloquent appreciation of Mom and a sensitive rendering of the poems selected by her granddaughter, enabling me to weep freely from beginning to end. But my father, who all his life had been easily moved to tears, and especially by poetry, sat beside me dry-eyed as he recited from memory the ancient prayers. At the time, I'd thought him supported by that remarkable stoic acceptance that had served him for nearly a century, or else too dazed to weep. But now I wondered if he refused to cry because he didn't believe that Mom had died.

"Do you see her too?"

"No. I only hear her."

"What does she say?"

He was silent, gazing over my shoulder intently, head slightly tilted, as if he were struggling to hear. When I prodded him to tell me, he found it difficult to convey. Finally he said, "I hear her addressing our group."

"What group?"

"A group . . . of which . . . we are members."

"About what?"

"About . . . about . . . it's hard to express exactly. About how they got to be in the group. About who fit in where. About each one's standing in the group and how it isn't always exactly what it should be."

As I continued to query him, I could see him conscientiously striving to convey the complicated scene he'd overheard, watched him search for the precise words that could carry his difficult nuanced meaning. At one point the words *status* and *popularity,* concerns Mom had passed to her children at our adolescence, slipped into our exchange—whether introduced by Dad or by me I cannot say—but he immediately disclaimed them as misleading.

"Who else spoke?" I asked.

"No one," he said. "Just Dorothy. She was the leader."

I suspected he'd simply had a vivid dream, but the next morning at breakfast he said urgently, "Alix, I'd like you to arrange to see Dorothy as soon as you can," and I knew it had not been a dream. This time I simply nodded.

When we returned to his room, Dad asked if I would mind cutting his fingernails. These were the nails he had cleaned at least twice a day for most of his life, now grown long and clawlike. I found a nailclipper and took his hand in mine. His hands seemed huge for such a tiny man—now a mere five feet three and 96 pounds, though at one time he was five feet seven and 140. ("I have always envied men of stature," he wrote in his memoir, "although small men are reputed to be aggressive and pugnacious. This was true of a lawyer of small physique, named George Spooner. After I became a lawyer I happened to be in a courtroom in which Spooner and a lawyer about twice his size were in a heated argument which the judge was unable to quell. Spooner finally challenged the much larger lawyer to step outside where Spooner promised to knock his adversary's head off.") His hands were broad and veiny, with large knuckles and stubby fingers, rather like my own. Our veins, though unsightly in their prominence, were greatly appreciated by medics who had to take samples of our blood.

When I had finished clipping the nails of both his hands, he rested one on my arm, cleared his throat, and said, "I've been waiting to tell you that though I don't always thank you for each of the many kindnesses you do for me, I want you to know how much I appreciate every one of them."

"Oh, no, Daddy," I protested, hoping to stop him, "you needn't thank me. I'm just grateful that I'm able to do it. I do it because I love you."

"Nevertheless," insisted my father in his soft, formal, yet

caressing voice, "I want you to know how much I appreciate all that you do for me."

Then we sat together in his room holding hands, as we smiled and wept.

*

Dad was eighty-four when he first blacked out and fell to the sidewalk en route to his office. That fall, so alarming to him, propelled him into abrupt semiretirement. Since most of his arbitration hearings at distant factories required that he rent a car at the airport, and he was afraid of a blackout on the highway that might endanger lives, after that he accepted only those assignments that did not require driving.

Soon he was falling every year, then several times a year. But though he banged up his back, his head, his hips, his thighs, his arms, and sprained his wrists, covering himself with alarming bruises, after his first fall he somehow (all that milk he'd drunk? his nine decades of speediness?) escaped breaking his bones. "It's nothing much," he would say dismissively when I called him after a fall, or "it hurts but it seems to be getting better." Still, I knew that eventually one of his falls was bound to be serious.

Then one day, six months after Mom died, as he was about to turn ninety-five, he took a fall in the dining room that fractured his right shoulder. The emergency room doctors considered him too old to survive the surgery required to set the bone and instead sent him home with his arm in a sling and the hope that it would heal on its own.

It didn't. So great was his pain and agitation that he kept pulling off his sling. Unable to feed himself with his left hand, he gradually stopped eating, despite his aide's attempts to feed him.

Nevertheless, we went ahead with plans for a birthday celebration for the Sunday closest to his ninety-fifth birthday, when all his grandchildren and great-grandchildren planned to fly in. I reserved one of Judson's public rooms and ordered Dad's favorite cake, chocolate with coconut frosting.

As the day approached, he grew worse. In his pain he soon required continuous morphine. After that, when I phoned, he barely spoke to me, and four nights before the scheduled party his nurse hinted that the end might be near.

Frantic, I phoned Dr. Murphy. "Do you think he's going to die?" I asked.

"Not tonight," said Dr. Murphy.

He'd snapped back so many times, it was hard to believe he wouldn't come back again. But I flew to Cleveland early the next morning.

When I arrived, he was in a morphine daze. "Hi, Daddy," I said, leaning close to his better ear, "I'm here."

He opened his eyes for a moment and mouthed, "Hi," though no sound came out. I took his hand and sat with him the rest of the day while the nurses turned him over on schedule, took his vital signs, tried to feed him a bit of food and drink. He opened his eyes each time I asked him to, but only for a second. "I love you, Daddy," I said in his ear, and his lips mouthed back, "I love you."

The next day his eyes remained closed, but his big hand clutched mine tightly as I sat beside him. When I swabbed his parched lips, he rooted like an infant searching for the nipple and took some sips of liquid food, then returned to sleep. All day I watched him breathe. His breath was labored and irregular. At one point he thrashed his legs and said in a whispery voice, "I want to go to the washroom."

But it was too late, and instead his nurse changed him. Though I didn't know it, those were the last words uttered by that fastidious man.

Had I made it to his side just in time? Or did my presence free him to depart? By midafternoon the nurses were unable to get any blood pressures, though he continued his labored noisy breathing. The intervals between breaths lengthened until, in the late afternoon, seven months to the day after Mom had died, his eyes opened to meet mine, and then there were no more breaths. "Daddy, Daddy," I called, but he was gone.

Afterward, I understood that during those two unforgettable days I had been engaged in the ancient vigil known as "deathwatch." Months before, I had thought myself lucky to have been spared the agony of witnessing my mother's death; now I knew it was my misfortune. My true luck—my blessing—is to have witnessed my father's: to have held his ancient sinewy hand, spoken my love into his better ear, watched his eyes flicker open to meet mine one last time before falling forever closed, breathed with him that loud, deep, drawn-out final breath.

At the gathering at my cousin's house following Dad's funeral, Johnny and I reminisced about our childhoods, particularly about the raisins, Chiclets, and sticks of gum Dad gave us as love tokens and rewards. Johnny thought they were sticks of Beeman's Pepsin, but I remembered—and knew Bob would have too—that they were Wrigley's Spearmint.

In the rental car on the way to the airport, as I opened the glove compartment to clear it out, to my astonishment I found beneath the rental contract a single stick of Wrigley's

Spearmint gum wrapped in its foil wrapper. My children and husband are my witnesses.

I took it as a sign from Dad that he was pleased with the way I'd handled things seeing him out of this world. With the gum in my purse and a mourner's candle in my bag, I flew back to New York.

The Shaker house

Afterword

A year after my mother died, *Memoirs of an Ex-Prom Queen,* which had once scandalized my hometown, was reissued in a twenty-fifth-anniversary edition that took me back to Cleveland for some readings. As I had an extra hour before the rental car was due back at the airport and it was a brilliant May Sunday morning, I decided to drive past the Shaker house once more.

As I slowed to a stop, I was shocked to see how much had changed in the few months since my parents had left the world: a winter storm had taken down the last remaining elm, leaving the great lawn bare; the wooden trim, most of which Dad had kept brown, a color that requires infrequent painting, was now white; and the entire house was crowned with a shimmering new roof.

Unable to tear myself away, I parked the car and walked up the drive. A giant middle-aged man came around the house to meet me. He wore overalls and carried a trowel. "Is there something I can do for you?" he said in a forbidding British accent. "Doctor?" I replied, thrusting out my hand and introducing myself as the daughter of the former owners. Instead of apologizing for my Sunday intrusion and retreating down the drive, I waited to be invited inside, as Mom would have done.

The doctor kindly complied. He took me on a tour of

the house, proudly displaying all the work that he and his wife had done. The carpets were gone, revealing pristine hardwood floors. The kitchen was in the process of being stripped and renovated. The back entrance had been repositioned near the porch and the kitchen door sealed off. The summer porch had been winterized. Upstairs, Mom's closet had been captured to make space for a jacuzzi in the adjacent bathroom, and her dressing room/studio converted to a closet. My grandmother's rooms over the garage, originally built as servants' quarters, were now offices for the doctor's wife. Electronic devices enhanced every room. The vast third floor had been transformed into a gym with all the latest exercise equipment. All the walls had been repainted lively colors: the living room a designer pink, the hallways pale rose, the bedrooms green, blue, lavender, and cream. The biggest surprise was the room I'd always slept in—now a cheerful nursery for the doctor's new baby, with stenciled walls, a crib, a bassinet, and a veritable menagerie of stuffed animals.

At first sight my eyes revolted at the changes, as if my parents' pasts were being violated, their memory destroyed. Lucky for them, I thought, not to see their home desecrated by strangers.

Then I remembered Mom saying that if she were to do it again she would furnish the house differently—not with antiques but in a contemporary style. She would probably approve of the changes (she'd certainly applaud the new kitchen), and Dad wouldn't care one way or another, as long as he didn't have to foot the bill.

"You need only claim the events of your life to make yourself yours. When you truly possess all you have been and done, which may take some time, you are fierce with reality," wrote the octogenarian playwright Florida Scott-Maxwell.

As I followed the doctor back down the stairs, a memorial I'd recently attended for a friend's mother flashed to mind. To the assembled mourners my friend had described waking up one morning shortly after his mother's death inexplicably full of joy. "I couldn't understand it," he said. "There I was, a man who had just lost his mother—and yet I was happy. How could this be?" And not only happy, he said; he was filled with a prodigious rush of energy. Then he understood that when he'd opened his eyes that morning his mother's presence had entered him. Somehow she had infused him with her energy and washed him with happiness. From then on, he said, he was never without her.

I recognized that what my friend described was Scott-Maxwell's fierce jolt of reality. How often it now came over me: each time I opened my father's pocket watch to check the hour or brazenly wore my mother's mink; in fact, whenever I looked into the mirror. Having so long defined myself by our difference, I would once have cringed to see my parents' faces looking out at me. But now, when we are as distinct as life and death, it pleases me. Hearing Mom's easy laughter in my throat, feeling Dad's gestures in my hands, surrounded in my New York loft by their effects—the cloisonné honeymoon lamp, the framed portrait of Bob, Dad's Crystal Owl, Mom's Nevelson, and, yes, my stick of Wrigley's Spearmint gum—I know better who I am. The powers those objects embody, which I've fed upon since birth—Mom's sensuality and will, Dad's rationality and focus—are, like my parents themselves, the source of what I am.

But who were they? Though I've squinted through the keyhole at their past, read their private letters and manuscripts, I still can't say. Not only because my self-regard kept me ignorant of their lives but because like every parent they presented personae designed to protect now their children, now themselves. My deepest knowledge of them is as biased, partial, and self-serving as my knowledge of my brother Bob. The documents I hoped would reveal them to me confirmed their energy and optimism but kept their secrets. How could it be otherwise? How can one peer through the windows of one's parents' lives without encountering one's own opaque reflection?

As the doctor led me out the back door through the garden (where he'd been digging up Mom's roses to replant near the garage), I got a strong whiff of Mom's lilacs, which had burst into violent bloom. All at once, the sweet fragrance reminded me of what Carola de Florent, my parents' friend and neighbor, wrote to me after their deaths: "Each had a specific and intense sweetness which I describe to myself as the essence of intelligence. I doubt that you will quite accept my word. No child could. There is too much exchange of power between parent and child for the term sweetness to fit comfortably." Yet now that their power is spent, I taste their sweetness.

Yes, it was fitting, I concluded, that the house they had exuberantly inhabited for forty years should be again, in Dad's final judgment of Mom, "so full of life." Suddenly fierce with my new reality, I clasped the doctor's hand with Dad's grip and held his eyes with Mom's gaze and, speaking for us all, wished his family the complicated pleasures of long life.

Alix Kates Shulman is the author of ten previous books. She has taught at universities throughout the country, and her stories and essays have appeared in *The Atlantic Monthly, The Nation, Ms., The Women's Review of Books, Dissent,* and *The New York Times,* among other publications. She divides her time between New York City and Maine.

6/04	DATE DUE	
DEC 0 3 2004		